Lessons From a
21st-Century
One-Room
Schoolhouse

Lessons From a

21st-Century One-Room Schoolhouse

Patricia Huey

ISBN 979-8-218-40496-3

Published by Dunn Mountain Books in the United States of America.

Dunn Mountain Books
Summit Valley, Washington

Disclaimer: I have tried to recreate events, locales, and conversations from my memories of them. In order to maintain their anonymity, in some instances I have changed the names of individuals and places, I may have changed some identifying characteristics and details such as physical properties, occupations, and places of residence.

Dedication

To Justin, an overcomer, and the reason for it all.

To the Hill Creek directors, teachers,
therapists, parents, and students who are courageously
shaping the 21st Century through homeschooling.

And to Academy Northwest for
your vision for homeschoolers.

"It's not what you accomplish, but how faithful you are in what God calls you to do."

—TOMMIE CASEY BEATY

Table *of* Contents

Acknowledgments

Many thanks to the Pond and Parchment Guild for your helpful critiques and edits and for encouraging me to complete this project. A special thanks to Cher for our Zoom meetings where we kick around ideas "Inklings" style, keeping me focused by offering valuable insights when writer's block hits. Also, a heartfelt thank you to Linda, who has encouraged me in my teaching, writing, and spiritual walk over many years. Finally, thank you to Jesse and Amy for scheduling and hosting our writers' group meetings. What would we do without you?

Preface

SOME SAY YOU can't relive the past, but I believe we do through our memories.

This story is about a small Christian homeschool program I founded in Western Washington. Though atypical, Hill Creek Christian, a private school for homeschoolers, looms large among its students and teachers. I tell this story so that any parent who entertains the idea of homeschooling might be encouraged to obey the calling.

The school proved that "necessity is the mother of invention." Our son was born with mild cerebral palsy and some learning difficulties. Although we tried to make it work, the traditional school was not meeting his needs. And because of his need for a unique approach, the local Christian schools in our area were unable to educate him.

I prayed for direction and was led to Academy Northwest, a private school for homeschoolers with several learning centers around Washington State. Their program supported me in starting Hill Creek.

Hill Creek Christian was designed as a preparatory school for homeschoolers, including students with learning differences, using a one-room school model that I had researched. Its goal continues to be partnering with homeschooling parents in their children's education. Students with academic challenges were included in the regular classroom, and when appropriate, they were granted accommodations or modifications. The first few classes were in my home, but within a short time, it was necessary to find a larger space.

In 1996, two years after HCC launched, our family moved sixty miles north from Kirkland to Mount Vernon, Washington. I was amazed when parents were willing to make the trek north once or twice a week.

Seven years into the school's beginning, with forty-five students, I realized I could not teach every class that parents and students requested. I hoped to find a science teacher. A parent recommended Amorah Nelson, who had recently married into their family and was finishing her Master's degree. When she came to my home to interview, I knew she was perfect for the job.

In the early years of the school, we met in a small, renovated barn on our property, which some called "The Little Red Schoolhouse." Initially, high school classes were taught on Mondays and Wednesdays, with middle and elementary school on Tuesdays and Thursdays.

A while later, the students asked to change the school's name from Kingsgate Learning Center to something more updated. They collected possible names and then voted. Hill Creek Christian was the new name. One of the students, who worked for a graphic design business, created the HCC logo, which the school has used since.

When we outgrew The Little Red Schoolhouse, we moved the high school group to a church location nearby. Later, we moved to Emmanuel Baptist Church in Mount Vernon.

Hill Creek won the Academy Northwest Academic Excellence award for the first time in 2002. That distinction is awarded to the learning center with the highest test scores and most college scholarships earned. Our students have been selected as valedictorians numerous times at the Academy Northwest High School graduations, which all learning centers attend. Over the years, HCC has continued to win the Academic Excellence Award. It is no secret that the school has been blessed with many dedicated and committed parents, talented teachers, and students.

Hill Creek Christian welcomes all types of learners, and that model has benefitted countless students and families. Think of a bell curve. Stanine 5 runs through the middle of the bell curve from top to bottom. 5 is average. Stanine 6, 7, 8, and 9 are to the right of the bell curve. Those students are considered above average. They have been gifted with the ability to pick up information easily when taught using traditional methods. The students whose scores fall to the left of the bell curve in stanine 4, 3, and below exhibit a learning deficit; some may even have multiple deficits. HCC is unique because students with learning challenges are included in the regular classroom. Dedicated teachers modify and accommodate when test scores indicate such adjustments would be beneficial.

Educational therapy through the National Institute for Learning Development, which HCC implements, is critical to inclusion's success. The main goal of NILD Educational Therapy is the development of clear, efficient thinking. Educational therapists are different from tutors. Tutoring helps sharpen skills in specific subject areas. Educational therapists, on the other hand, skillfully pinpoint the student's individual deficits. Various carefully selected techniques are implemented twice weekly to target the deficient areas.

For example, one young man began educational therapy as a ninth grader. His Type 1 diabetes caused health problems and difficulties in the classroom due to lack of sleep from nighttime high blood sugars. After one successful year of educational therapy, he enrolled in HCC while continuing therapy. Accommodations were granted, and he thrived, rising to the top of his classes. Naturally determined, he became a top student and was selected as a teacher's assistant. He completed educational therapy in his junior year. He was nominated for the National Honor Society and was presented with the Student of the Year award. This type of success is not atypical for struggling learners at HCC due to the NILD program, high expectations, and dedicated teachers willing to invest time in those students who might be overlooked in other academic settings. Recently, I received a text message from this student. He was happy to announce that he had been accepted into a nursing program where his concentration would be working with people diagnosed with diabetes.

I stepped down as co-director to care for my mother, and Amorah continued the work. I continued as a therapist. Eventually, the number of Hill Creek educational therapists increased to three. Those dedicated teacher-therapists paid for their expensive training out of pocket.

Hill Creek has always been about Kingdom work. HCC's mission statement is "To know Christ and make Him known through Christian education." The school continues to fill a need for homeschool families in Western Washington's Skagit Valley and surrounding counties with Amorah Nelson's leadership.

While this brief history offers the reader an overview of HCC, I pray it conveys the true heart of the school. I invite you to enter the school's beginning stages and experience its soul and spirit through the following scenarios and vignettes.

CHAPTER 1

Pure Gold

"All things are ready, if our mind be so."

—WILLIAM SHAKESPEARE, HENRY V

The Preparation

SWEAT DROPLETS TICKLED my scalp, but I resisted scratching. Instead, I placed my hands on the table. To my horror, they were visibly shaking, so I jammed them into my lap. I considered standing, thanking everyone, and bowing out, but I was desperate for this job since our son was in an expensive private school for kids with learning disabilities.

The panel of five across the large table neither smiled nor frowned, causing my panic to soar. The round of interview questions began, and my stomach turned upside down. Then, to my relief, one person, a nondescript lady with brown hair and dark eyes, smiled—a lifeline tossed my way. I calmed down.

Back home, I pounced on the phone each time it rang, but the only calls I received were from friends. Negative self-talk set in. I had never felt qualified for the job, even though my credentials spoke otherwise.

The phone rang. "Hello?"

"This is HR. Congratulations! You were selected for the Adult Basic Ed position. Looks like Monday morning is your start date!"

Flooded with relief, all I could manage was a grateful "Thank you!"

The job was at the local community college, about ten minutes from our home. I liked the idea of the ABE program. People who tested for a particular program but failed to meet the standards for regular college-level 101 classes were directed to the learning lab to increase their skills. Most were motivated because they needed a higher-paying job. I certainly understood that!

My immediate supervisor, Judy Kenner, was the lady on the interview panel who smiled at me. She was a small bird-like woman, likely in her late 50s. She wore large glasses, a dark skirt, a maroon blouse, and a black cardigan that seemed too large for her frame. She was rather plain, and in my prideful youth, I hoped she'd be able to train me adequately.

I had no idea what I was in for.

On Monday morning, Judy showed me my desk, which sat adjacent to hers. I noticed it was the best location in the room. Someone had sharpened pencils and placed them with various colored pens in a holder next to a large desk calendar. There was a yellow envelope on the desk with my name on it.

I opened it, and it read, "You are the best person for this job. If you weren't, you would not have been hired. I can't wait to see you transform lives." Judy had signed it. I looked up, but Judy moved on and motioned to me. I dashed over, eager to please.

Judy transformed from bird-like to professional in the blink of an eye. She calmly fired information at me like a Gatling gun, and I wrote down as much as possible on a flip pad. I had a gut feeling that anything that came out of her mouth was important.

By lunch, I'd memorized the passcode for the computers, met with sixty students, enrolled three new students, sat through Judy's English class, learned how to keep student records, perused curriculum, organized small groups, and shadowed Judy as she tutored struggling students. I was exhausted and hungry by 12:30 and hoped to grab lunch and coffee. My boss sprinted back to her desk. I dragged behind her.

"I like to bring my lunch to work," she said, unscathed from the taxing morning. Otherwise, I can't stick to WeightWatchers. *Was she a WeightWatcher? This tiny little lady?* She offered me half her sandwich and a paper cup.

"I'll split with you. I don't like to waste time, and we can talk over lunch if you don't mind." She poured some coffee into my cup.

"I like to use real bread," she said, as if I'd inquired about it. "If you use that other stuff, the low-calorie kind, you'll starve by the end of the day. What do you think about low-calorie bread?"

"Well, I haven't really thought much about it." I'd just turned 39, and up until then, I hadn't thought much about cutting calories.

"I think quality speaks for itself whether it's bread or anything else." I didn't know it yet, but that was my first lesson.

After lunch, I attended two meetings, taught a math class, and tutored six future nursing students.

At 3:30, the last students trickled out of the learning lab. I hobbled over to my desk, my back aching. I made a mental note to wear more practical shoes the next day.

"Successful day today! It certainly wasn't as hectic as a typical Monday!" she said. I tried to imagine typical. "Let me show you how to sign out. I like to arrive and leave on time, so I can get to the Y."

Good grief! She worked out at the Y after a grueling day! This was no typical lady.

The ensuing days proved much more hectic than that first exhausting day, but my stamina improved after a few weeks. I could finally keep up with Judy reasonably well, and if I followed her lead, ate right, and exercised, I could keep up the demanding pace.

She introduced me to new responsibilities each week but always led by example. She warmly endorsed me to her students, and I learned her tricks of the trade. I had never known a master teacher until now.

I noticed that she was always honest with the students and with me. One day, I overheard a conversation between her and a welding student, a man about fifty, who'd lost his job a few months before enrolling in the technical program.

"Andy, you might not like what I'm going to tell you, but hear me out. Your scores are not quite where I want them to be. I can't endorse you for the program yet, but if you continue to work as hard as you have the past eight weeks, I guarantee you'll be ready for the next start date. I'll stay with you every step of the way."

"But the program doesn't start for three months! I have a family to support!"

"That's good motivation. You're as strong on the inside as you are on the outside! You can do it!" Her enthusiasm and confidence spilled over. I watched Andy perk up. I knew he'd make it into the next class.

One day, a newly hired teacher joined us. On the one hand, I was grateful that we'd have more help, but on the other hand, I felt a little jealous that I'd have to share Judy. The other teacher was outgoing and confident. What if Judy favored her?

As time passed and Lynn, the excellent new teacher, settled in, I watched Judy mentor and encourage her. A bond formed between them, as it had between Judy and me. I realized that a bond had developed among the three of us.

I marveled that Judy almost effortlessly continued to work with me, too, even though her schedule was impossibly tight. To my relief, she didn't appear to compare Lynn and me. She seemed to genuinely respect our "unique" abilities, as she called them.

Somehow, she knew what I valued most in education. Since my son had disabilities, I cared deeply about struggling learners. Including those students in my "regular" classes was essential to me—but it was not a popular concept due to budgeting. However, Judy seemed to value my philosophy.

One morning, she walked to my desk and sat down. I was frantically trying to finish prepping for a class, but when Judy spoke, I'd learned to stop what I was doing, knowing she must have something important to share.

"What do you think about pursuing tenure?"

"Tenure?" Stunned, I watched her pull papers out of a book bag.

"Yes. I'd like to see you develop your idea of inclusion. You're mastering your craft, and I'd like to see you create something to add to our program." She put the paperwork on my desk. Fill this out and bring it back in the morning." She smiled, stood up, and walked over to a waiting student.

I considered shouting the news to everyone within hearing distance, but I thought better. I called my husband instead.

"Guess what?" I practically shouted into the phone.

"Must be something good."

"I'm going to work toward tenure! Judy thinks I'm ready!"

"Sounds like work to me. But congrats!"

Yes, I'd work hard because Judy would set the pace. Even so, I felt confident I'd achieve my goals. I'd always been a little bit of a lone wolf, but Judy had taught me the value of teamwork. I floated through that day, ready for the challenges ahead. My boss was a rare bird with no intentions of clipping my wings.

Throughout the long tenure process, Judy sacrificed her time. I learned she was no run-of-the-mill "top-down" boss but a servant leader who encouraged me to put forth my best effort despite obstacles. Time was our enemy every day, and with the extra work of the tenure process, Judy's patient persistence inspired me to persevere.

While Judy was one of the most compassionate people I knew, she was not soft. I learned that compassion takes many forms, and sometimes compassion presents as hardcore. On more than one occasion, I watched her stick to her convictions, whether it was about a new program she did not see a need for or a new curriculum that she felt would not prove beneficial.

While at the learning center, I transformed my abilities like a fledgling eagle learning from its parent while still in the nest. And like the fledgling, I eventually outgrew it.

About three years later, I approached Judy.

"Want to grab some lunch today?" My question was more of a plea than a request.

"What's up?" We knew each other well by now.

As we ate our salads, I broached the subject. "Judy, I have the opportunity to start a school using the academic inclusion model."

"I figured you'd leave sooner or later. It doesn't make it easy, though. It's always hard for me to lose good people." I noticed she pushed her salad aside. "Of course, you're ready for the challenge."

Over the next twenty-five minutes, I outlined my ideas. She listened without interrupting.

She pulled her salad back over and picked at it. "I endorse your plan. Let me know how I can help."

Like an eagle, I flew out of the nest and soared. Using the work ethic Judy had instilled in me, I could start the school I was called to. The standards at the school were Judy's. They flowed from her to me, into our school's enthusiastic teachers, and from there to the parents and students.

Over the years, I took Judy's example to the next generation. Her attitude of "I'm the boss, but I'm also a teacher like you" prepared me to take her philosophy to others who caught her vision, too.

Looking back, I realize you can look at a package but don't know what you've got unless you open it. When I first met Judy, I figured she was an ordinary boss who told her employees what to do from an "off-limits" office. But Judy invited me to unwrap the gift of herself, and I found that what was inside was pure gold. Who could have known I'd be so fortunate to glean so much from one incredible teacher?

Years later, I'm now retired from the school I founded. And Judy's high standards and integrity? If you look carefully, you'll see them written into teachers' lesson plans, in students' homework, and on the faces of graduating seniors as they carry them into the world.

Of course, at that time, I had yet to experience what the future would bring. I now realize that God doesn't give us a task without preparing us for it. Here is the story of how it happened.

CHAPTER 2

A Calling

*"Faith is taking the first step even when
you don't see the whole staircase."*

—Martin Luther King, Jr.

JUST A FEW days before my lunch conversation with Judy about starting a school of inclusion, I had a surprise phone call from the director of a fully accredited and state-approved school for homeschoolers—Academy Northwest. I had been searching for a program that would benefit our son, Justin.

I ended that call, sensing that a major shift was happening. The director had encouraged me to teach other homeschoolers besides my son, something I had yet to consider. Have you ever experienced a moment when you knew your life was about to change?

During our conversation, the Christian director informed me that a training class was required to become a certified homeschool teacher. I realized that if I followed through with training and signed a contract with ANW, I would start a new teaching career. I also realized that God had planted the seeds for my future as a teenager growing up in Alabama because of one memory.

* * *

Locals relish autumn in the South due to the more comfortable temperatures and lower humidity. I remember one fall day when bright-colored leaves splashed against a dazzling blue sky. On the drive home from school, I felt mixed emotions. I wanted to ride my bike the six blocks to the library, but I also knew I needed to get on my homework. If I didn't finish it, I wouldn't be able to hear the guest speaker that evening. Lillian Williamson, a missionary to China and home on leave, was speaking at the monthly potluck supper, and I wanted to hear what she had to say. I made my decision to skip the bike ride.

That evening, everyone gathered at church. Dinner smells permeated the fellowship hall, with multiple conversations and much laughter. I observed Mrs. Williamson talking to a small group by the kitchen. She was of average height and had salt-and-pepper hair. She wore glasses and seemed shy. She looked up and smiled at me from across the room, and I felt an instant connection.

After dinner, I found one of the last seats in the front row. Mrs. Williamson smiled warmly. "Someone told me you play hymns. Would you mind playing a couple tonight?"

Panic-stricken, I tried to utter a "no," but something about her made me say, "Yes, ma'am, but I'm not good with sharps without practice."

She laughed and threw her arm around my shoulder as if she'd known me all my life. "I never was either! These both have flats!" She handed me the hymnal with the pages marked and with far more confidence in my abilities than I had. I'd always struggled with confidence, although I tried to keep it a secret.

After the two hymns, she began her presentation, and her shy persona vanished. As she spoke, I saw her heart. Her one desire was to lead lost sheep into the fold.

Her presentation excited me. Did God have something like this in store for me? Was I being called to the mission field? If so, I knew I wanted to go. My response was not capricious, which might be expected from a fifteen-year-old high school freshman.

After the presentation, I waited to speak with Mrs. Williamson. Finally, it was my turn. I told her I longed to go to the mission field. As if I was the only person in the room, she said, "The road to the mission field is long and bumpy. If you're truly called, you'll continue down the path no matter the obstacles." Although her words sounded like a warning, I went home that night with direction and conviction. I knew where I was headed. Or so I thought.

Several years later, I'd completed my degree in education and was married to a military guy. Even though I never forgot that night at the church back home in Alabama, my life seemed to be heading in a direction of its own with many cares and concerns.

When our son was two years old, we noticed he wasn't talking as much as other toddlers his age. Although he had walked on time, his gait was off. We decided to get him checked out. We received the diagnosis of a neurological impairment and mild cerebral palsy, along with a language and auditory delay.

Like all parents, we had looked forward to our son's birth and a future of blessings as we would watch him grow up, become educated, follow the Lord, get married, and have his own children.

But we realized all our hopes and dreams might not come to fruition. We were initially devastated by the diagnosis. But we were young and hopeful, and we vowed to make the best of the situation, which we did throughout many military transfers.

My husband, Steve, was stationed at Sand Point near Seattle in Washington State when our son was twelve years old. From past experience, I knew finding the right school would be pretty difficult. And I was right. Since his initial evaluation, he had been tested many times, with similar results. Justin needed a unique academic situation.

After yet another public school enrollment, we decided he needed a better placement. We had heard about a private school for kids with disabilities, so we enrolled him, knowing that the tuition would put a tight squeeze on our budget. But we didn't know what else to do.

One day, while walking on the track, I talked to a friend about it. Cheryl, who was homeschooling her kids, stressed that Justin needed a different approach to learning. She suggested that I explore homeschooling and even suggested starting a school. I thought she was a little crazy at the time. One thing she stressed that made perfect sense to me was that homeschooling would allow Justin to learn at his own pace.

I researched homeschooling and found that Washington State had solid homeschool laws. I figured I could homeschool Justin, but I knew I wanted to be part of an organization—not alone. As I looked into available co-ops, I stumbled across Academy Northwest and what seemed like excellent homeschool opportunities and support. I was impressed that the organization was fully accredited and approved by Washington State, so the requirements to graduate would be the same as those of the public school system.

I needed to pray about this decision. Steve thought it would be a good move even though I was making a good salary at the local community college. If I homeschooled Justin, though, we would not be paying tuition. We wouldn't worry so much about finances. Of course, my 401(K) would go away. But what was more important?

In my heart, I felt I was drifting farther away from the mission field. But God can always turn the impossible into possible, and I was about to experience that first-hand.

CHAPTER 3

A Different Approach

*"Security is mostly a superstition. Life is
usually a daring adventure or nothing."*

—HELEN KELLER

WHEN THE DIRECTOR of Academy Northwest returned my call inquiring about their program, she explained it in detail, and almost everything made sense to me. As I mentioned, I hung up on that call, feeling like my life was about to take a new direction. But something was nagging me—something I had been ignoring.

When something bothered me, I'd often drive up to the track near our home and walk around it eight times. During the two-mile walk, I could usually work things out. Sometimes, I walked with a friend, but today, it was just God, me, and the drizzling rain.

On lap one, I told God I felt unsettled. I wanted to move forward with the learning center idea. I knew I had to leave my job and a good salary, but something else was bothering me. The ANW program was primarily a homeschooling program, and although it did offer credit recovery for adults, my main focus would be working with homeschooling parents and students. At that time, my view of homeschoolers was inaccurate, incomplete, and somewhat skewed by my public education background.

During lap two, I prayed, "God, here I am about to sign up with a program where I'll work with homeschoolers, people with huge families all wearing the same denim outfit. You know, the granola types. I've been told that homeschoolers won't be able to make it in the real world. They just aren't socialized enough."

On lap three, a thought ran through my mind. *Homeschoolers often win the National Spelling Bee. And what about National History Day? You must admit that you've noticed that* homeschooled *kids at church are personable, helpful, and articulate well with each other and adults. They seem pretty social.*

About half way through my walk, I prayed more, "Lord, why do parents homeschool to begin with? I feel slightly confused because the homeschooling parents I've talked to all have differing views. It seems there is no standard answer."

On lap five, I had another thought. *You have your reasons for considering this* homeschooling *program, and others have theirs. Parents don't have the same reasons for* homeschooling, *but all of them are seeking academic freedom.*

Around lap six, another thought came to mind. *You left the K-12 system for the community college job because you had felt unsettled. Yes, it was about needing more income, but it was more than that. Your problem hadn't been with the teaching or with your colleagues. It had been at the federal and state levels, and you disagreed with the new, progressive ideas.*

Nearing the end of lap seven, I told God, "I've considered this path in the first place because of Justin. Will this be the best for him? I know what doctors, teachers, neurologists, and other professionals have predicted-- that he will not progress. We never believed that, and he has progressed in many areas well beyond what they thought. This plan is way outside the box, though! But what we're currently doing is not working well, so shouldn't I pursue this new path? Just to let you know, I feel like I'm stepping off a cliff."

On my last lap, one final thought ran through my mind. *Justin needs a different approach to learning. And what if others could benefit, as well? And not just kids with learning differences. What about typical kids? Or even the accelerated ones?*

The drizzle had stopped, and the sun shone as I strolled to my car. A cloud had lifted, and I felt more at peace. I breathed a shallow prayer. "Stay with me, Lord. Please work out the details as I travel down this path."

* * *

The Academy Northwest teacher certification training day arrived, and I looked forward to it even though I was nervous. As always, fear reared its annoying head, and as usual, I beat it down as best I could.

The efficient director greeted our small class of teachers, and we immediately opened a three-ring binder filled with interesting information.

Her first assignment asked the teachers to give at least one reason for wanting certification in teaching homeschoolers. The answers were as diverse as they were interesting.

A frustrated teacher said she had decided to leave her position in search of students who wanted to learn and behave. She was weary of disciplining more than she was teaching. Almost every teacher was looking for a faith-based approach. One desired to use Christian curriculum exclusively. Two of them had been homeschooling their children and wanted to join other teachers in the Academy Northwest program. I was drawn to one teacher, in particular, who planned to select a curriculum based on each of her student's individual needs. What a concept! Finally, it was my turn to share, and I told them about our experience in traditional school with Justin and how I was looking for a program where he could learn at his own pace without being labeled.

The next part of our training clarified homeschooling laws, and I was especially intrigued that the director had lobbied for Washington's homeschool laws throughout the years.

The director asked us to jot down our homeschooling plans and goals for our learning centers. I explained my desire to start a school of inclusion. She collected them and shared them with the class.

The director looked at me and said, "You're in the right place." And I believed her.

Next, she lectured on how to run a learning center from a business standpoint. Since I had never taken business classes in college, her wealth of knowledge and ideas about how to structure the business proved essential.

Finally, she introduced us to Academy Northwest homeschooling parents and students. There was no matching denim or granola in sight. One couple did have a large family, and I found them delightful. Homeschoolers, parents, and their children, who addressed us, were articulate, engaging, and witty.

Later that day, I headed out to the track. Again, it was just God and me.

During the eight laps, my decision to work with homeschoolers was confirmed. I knew God had directed me to Academy Northwest, and I felt excited and determined. I thanked Him for answering all my questions at the training session and guiding me to homeschool. At last, I knew beyond the shadow of a doubt that I was on the right path.

Now, I needed to get serious about planning. Fall was right around the corner.

CHAPTER 4

Getting Started

"Creativity is intelligence having fun."

−ALBERT EINSTEIN

STRUCTURING MY LEARNING center served a few purposes other than my own. The director stressed helping the parents by making myself available to assist them with curriculum choices, teaching techniques, and tips, as well as teaching one or two subjects. I knew from prior experience that relationships trump when it comes to parents and students; therefore, I designed a schedule that I hoped would work for everyone. I planned to teach a two-and-a-half-hour class in English grammar, essay writing, and literature with a history link. In the first year, I would teach American literature and U.S. history. In the second year, I would teach world literature linked with world history. The high school classes would be held on the first three Tuesdays of the month from 9:00 to noon. I would meet with everyone individually on the fourth week of the month for one and a half hours each.

From the training session, I learned that I could expect my initial enrollment to be low. Since I wanted to spend adequate time teaching Justin, eight to ten students sounded fine. I would have plenty of time with the other homeschoolers since he had landed a part-time job at a Safeway near our home.

I enthusiastically planned my first semester classes and field trips. I was not worried that our house was small. I knew I could teach my small learning center at our kitchen table.

Almost immediately, though, I received multiple inquiries from interested parents! I explained class offerings and plans to each parent.

Just before school started in September 1994, I had enrolled twelve high school students and eight elementary and middle school students. With twenty students, I had a serious problem. I needed space to rent! And I would need to manage my time carefully, to give Justin adequate attention for his coursework.

Fortunately, I discovered I could reserve a room at the local library once weekly for up to three hours. The room was large enough for the students and parents who wanted to sit through the classes.

On Thursdays, I taught classes to the elementary and middle school students. We often engaged in experiential learning, visiting various exhibits and museums. I met individually with those students and parents one week of the month.

My husband reminded me often that I seemed to be working too much. I told him things would settle down once I had the learning center running smoothly. Teaching on Tuesdays and Thursdays, meeting individually with families, staying up late, planning, and correcting was tiring, but I felt great satisfaction working with such terrific families. I was amazed at how diligently the parents worked to educate their children, and the parents and I formed a bond I hadn't experienced before in my seventeen years of teaching.

I also enjoyed knowing I was steering Justin down the right academic path. He was already more self-confident and relaxed, and he could delve into U.S. history, his favorite subject, at a depth he had not had time to previously pursue. Would he overcome his obstacles? I was beginning to trust God on that—whatever the outcome.

Parents sent their tuition to Academy Northwest, where the accountant took a small percentage for the organization and sent the remaining amount to me. I had taken a considerable cut in pay to run my learning center, but I knew I was doing the right thing. This position felt more like a calling than a job.

Academy Northwest required their contracted teachers to attend faculty meetings once per quarter. I looked forward to the sessions because curriculum was on display, and curriculum writers frequently spoke at the meetings. Further, we learned how to refine our learning centers. Various teachers were sometimes responsible for instructing the faculty in one subject area, sharing teaching tips and techniques, and learning center experiences. I knew the day would come for me to teach these incredible colleagues, too. I shoved anxiety back, vowing not to worry. I had expertise in areas, too, I reminded myself.

The teachers presented as delightful, outside-the-box non-conformists. In the past, I'd been told that I was the epitome of a non-conformist, and I had found that a non-conformist's life is not always easy. But here I was in a group of teachers who spoke my language, the educational language of unconventional teachers who passionately pursued and perfected their craft.

* * *

The first year of my learning center passed quickly, and I looked forward to improving and refining it the following year.

In the learning center's second year, our focus was world literature. During the second semester, we read various Shakespeare sonnets and then Shakespeare's *As You Like It*. I asked the students if they would like to host a dinner theater for their parents as an end-of-the-year finale. The idea was an immediate hit, so I wrote a play titled Shakespeare: A Man for All Time. In the play, modern students, through a fluke, met and conversed with William Shakespeare. Humor and profound, reflective moments ensued, and every student, including the younger ones, played a part.

The students worked arduously to find props, even locating a smoke machine for when Shakespeare mysteriously appeared. They researched the Elizabethan age, searched thrift shops for costumes, researched time-period food, and created an appropriate menu for the event.

The problem was that I was feeling a little overwhelmed and exhausted. I worked day and night teaching classes, meeting individually with students, holding play practices, tracking down a venue for the night's event, helping parents with their year-end records, administering year-end achievement tests, and preparing food for the banquet. I felt the effects, but my pride kept me from admitting it even to myself.

The night of the event arrived, and the students entertained as professionals would. They quoted Shakespeare passages, performed short scenes from Shakespeare's plays, quizzed the visiting Shakespeare, and served their parents banquet food with aplomb. The event was a huge success. All the hard work had paid off.

As I attempted to recover the next day, a parent called to ask if I could meet with a small group of parents. I wondered what the meeting was about, but she said they just wanted to talk, so five moms came to my house the following Monday. They brought snacks and drinks, and we sat at my table, talked and laughed, and reminisced about the school year.

Then Janet spoke up. "We're here to tell you we want to help you."

"Help me?"

"Clearly, Patty, you are exhausted. The kids have learned much this year, and the banquet was fantastic. We didn't know our kids could perform in such an event. But why didn't you ask for help?"

I was at a loss for words. Finally, I mumbled, "Well, I figured it was my job."

"This is homeschooling. You are the lead. But we want you around for a while, okay? Next time, let us know where you need the help. We had no idea all that you'd planned. We could have brought food, set up the banquet room and stage, helped with props, anything. We're here for you."

I thanked them, feeling a little foolish. I was beginning to understand the homeschool culture more, and I liked it.

After they left, I realized I'd fallen into the "lone wolf" syndrome that likely came from being raised as an only child. Judy had warned against that and had always emphasized teamwork. I realized that I hadn't communicated my plans well nor delegated as I should have; therefore, I wore myself out, and it showed. I was embarrassed and vowed not to repeat that mistake.

I walked over to my chair and propped up my feet. I realized that God had used those parents to help me transition from my previous teaching models to homeschooling. While I had enjoyed working with parents in the past, most left their children's education fully up to me. In homeschooling, the parents were eager to learn what their kids were learning. They wanted to help me help their kids—an invaluable lesson.

I hadn't brought this up with the parents yet, but Steve and I had bought a house in Mount Vernon, about an hour north in the Skagit Valley, to be closer to my aging parents. I decided to tell the parents at their conferences the following week. We were only moving an hour north, but I worried an hour might be too far for some to drive. I cared deeply for these parents and students and hoped that we could work something out. I moved from my chair to the backyard to do a little weeding. I needed to think. There must be a solution to this problem. Maybe I could meet them halfway.

CHAPTER 5

The Little Red Schoolhouse

"God's work done in God's way will never lack God's supplies."

—Hudson Taylor

THE TWO OF us stood on the same scaffold on the west side of our new house—the high side. My dad, now in his early 70s, painted fast and furiously. Each time he slopped the roller into the tray, the scaffold shook like waves churning in a storm on the sea. As I clutched the platform with one hand, I carefully inched the other over to the tray and lowered my roller timorously into the paint to not rock the scaffold further. My head throbbed. I felt faint.

"Dad, I feel a little dizzy up here."

"Nonsense. Just keep your eyes on what you're doing."

For some idiotic reason, I glanced out towards the west and over the breadth of the rippling pond on our property. Vertigo forced me to cling with all my strength to the wobbly scaffold. My heart raced. I was perspiring and cold. *This is the stupidest thing I've ever done.*

I glanced at my father, who was painting up a storm. He certainly possessed admirable traits. Nothing scared him, really. He was driven, purposeful, and never gave up.

Because Steve was working, my dad had insisted on helping me paint the house we'd just moved into. "I'll be there at 8:00 in the morning, Pat!" he'd told me the night before. My dad was the only one who ever called me Pat.

"But, Dad, I don't think we should get on that scaffold. Maybe Steve and I should hire—"

"Nonsense!" The contractor left the scaffold there, so why not use it? You'll save some money!"

"But I'm a little afraid of, I mean, I worry about you—"

"Nonsense! What doesn't kill you will make you strong!"

"But dad—"

"See you at 8!"

So here we were, painting on the scaffold. Well, he was painting. I was clinging.

"Pat, your mom and I were talking last night. When are you going to get a real job? Don't you think you'd be happier teaching in a real school? What about Skagit Valley College? It's right here at your backdoor!"

Oh, so this was it. This was the real reason we were on the scaffold. I felt slightly irritated.

"What I'm doing IS real school, Dad. It's a lot harder than any job I've ever had!" I plunged my roller into the tray. The scaffold shook angrily, and I reminded myself to calm down.

"Well, it sure doesn't seem like it. Your mom and I were proud that you had a job at the college, making good money and having a good retirement. It's what we raised you to do. Do you even get paid for doing this new thing?"

"Well, of course, I get paid! And you didn't raise me to teach in a college, for Heaven's sake! And it was a community college. You make it sound like it was Harvard or something! You raised me to think for myself and work hard. Dad, I feel called to this. Nothing we have tried before has worked very well for Justin. And so far, this is. Think of him, okay?"

"Well, what the heck are we supposed to tell people when they ask what you're doing? Our daughter teaches kids in her home? Sounds like a daycare to me!"

"What's wrong with a daycare, Dad?"

I found that no matter how clearly I tried to convey my homeschool teaching, only some grasped the concept. It was both irritating and amusing to me. And right now, I felt annoyed with my dad. I appreciated his help and how he'd helped us fix up this old house. *Maybe he'll come around.* I shoved my roller into the paint tray. The scaffold shook.

* * *

"What do you think about turning the barn into a school?" I asked Steve. "I like the one-room school model where no kid is invisible and everyone is included. Teaching in my own one-room school would be awesome!"

We were on a week's vacation at the coast that June, but I couldn't fully enjoy the time away. Since the move from Kirkland, I'd been unable to find rental space for the learning center. Skagit Valley's Mount Vernon, Washington library didn't work as well as the one in Kirkland because it had too many limitations. I knew I could meet individually or in small groups in our home, but that wasn't the best model, either. I yearned for a real classroom. And the homeschooling parents were relying on me. I was both thrilled and humbled that they had all decided to make the drive north a couple of times a week.

"I suppose we could ask John for help," Steve said.

"Is that a yes, then?" Elated, I jumped up and did a little dance.

"Don't get too excited. We have to make sure he's available."

So, we called John, Steve's brother, to see if he'd fly from Alabama to help us transform the old barn into a classroom. He could build anything! I knew John's expertise would make the old barn look great.

"I'd do anything to get out of this heat! Just send me a ticket!" he'd said.

We talked to his wife, Hope, a nurse, who couldn't get away, but she was okay with the plan. I was grateful for her willingness. After all, they were raising two children, and she'd have to manage on her own.

Within a short time, John and Steve had transformed the old barn into a schoolroom with my dad's help.

"What color are you going to paint the outside?" John asked.

"Barn red," my dad answered, as if I hadn't been standing there. But I liked the idea.

* * *

Steve was busy painting the inside of the classroom. Dad and I were on ladders painting the outside.

"This looks like a real school," Dad remarked as he rolled red paint onto the exterior.

"Glad you think so, Dad."

"I went to a one-room schoolhouse growing up in Mississippi. Reminds me of that. But it's prettier here in the countryside with the farms and livestock all around."

"I never knew you went to a one-room school!"

"Well, I was there until eighth grade. It's funny. I liked playing basketball in high school, but those earlier years are what I remember. Funny how history repeats itself." He looked over at me.

"You missed a spot there, Pat."

"I see that, Dad."

* * *

With the inside painted, carpet laid, chalkboard hung, tables and bookshelves in, a projector screen installed, and textbooks arriving, I felt less anxious about the school year. It hadn't been easy or inexpensive.

I walked into the classroom and breathed in. I loved the new and old smells that melded to give the classroom its distinctive scent.

Thank you, God, for everything you've helped us accomplish this summer.

I decided to put up some posters and a couple of pictures. School was starting in a few days, and I was almost ready. With the families from Kirkland continuing and the new Mount Vernon enrollment, the school was expanding, but the new classroom offered plenty of space.

My dad clamored into the classroom carrying a large, framed picture. "Pat, will you hang the Norman Rockwell in here?" He turned the picture towards me.

In Rockwell's painting The School Teacher, the artist depicts a surprise party for Miss Jones, the schoolteacher. To me, this picture portrays the epitome of an American classroom. Children sit at their desks in neat rows. Humble gifts lay on the teacher's desk: a couple of apples, droopy flowers, and packages tied with string. "Happy Birthday, Jonesy" is scrawled on the blackboard. Rockwell includes an eraser with chalk dust on the floor, hinting at an eraser fight as the kids prepared for the surprise birthday party.

I cherished the print I'd found in an antique store years before and had it framed.

"No, I think I'd like it in the house in my office."

"Okay. I'll take it inside. Then I'm leaving for home."

"Thanks, Dad. Be careful driving."

Although he sometimes seemed a little extreme, I appreciated my dad's heart. He loved to help us, and we'd needed plenty for several weeks.

I thought about that day on the scaffold and smiled. I wondered who'd built that wobbly thing. I knew one thing for sure. I wouldn't have been on it if my father hadn't been with me.

And then it hit me. The Lord had given me a spiritual scaffold to start the learning center. It would need to be climbed, but it wouldn't be wobbly. At times, it might look different, but I shouldn't be fearful or embarrassed since my Heavenly Father was helping me achieve a difficult task.

I picked up the last poster. I hadn't known if I'd use it when I purchased it. On the left side was a photo of C.S. Lewis. Down the middle was a quote by him that struck me: "When the whole world is running towards a cliff, he who is running in the opposite direction appears to have lost his mind."

I hung it in the front and center of the classroom.

CHAPTER 6

A Birthday Lesson

"It is hard to fail, but it is worse never to have tried to succeed."

—THEODORE ROOSEVELT

ON THE FIRST day of class in September 1997, I walked from the house through the classroom door into the brightly decorated and well-equipped classroom. I had never had a shorter commute to work! With everything provided, I felt relief, gratitude, and excitement.

The projector sat on a table in front of a mounted screen. Textbooks lay near it, stacked neatly on my desk. I counted the chairs in front of rectangular tables one last time, checked to ensure all handouts were in the appropriate folders, and then glanced at the welcome to the students on the chalkboard. It read: *Welcome! You are 'fearfully and wonderfully made.' There is no other version of you. I hope to see you all prosper this school year!* Homeschooling is a privilege. Let's make the best of it! I heard a car pull up in the driveway and whispered a prayer.

* * *

It was now early October, and I looked forward to my teaching day. It was my birthday, and our family was celebrating that evening. Fourteen elementary-aged students ages seven through twelve would arrive in about an hour. The school had morphed into a couple of days of elementary, middle school, and high school classes each week. Today, I'd be teaching elementary/middle school level students. We focused on language arts and U.S. history. I also included vocabulary, grammar, and paragraph writing. Later in the school year, I would teach research writing, simple essays, and editing skills. I liked to tie the history we were studying with the literature units and the writing components. Integrated learning made sense to the students, and they thrived. The Christian curriculum we were using also allowed me to discuss spiritual issues as they came up.

Later in the day, we would work on math concepts. In addition to their grade-level curriculum, students memorized math facts, building fluency in math and other areas. Today, after weeks of work, there was a math facts competition.

I enjoyed the classroom energy generated from healthy competition. We had a store set up so prizes could be earned.

On certain days, we studied science, but I knew teaching science was not my strong suit or area of interest, and I was praying for a science teacher to join me for all grade levels. I needed a creationist who could teach all levels of science and didn't mind working hard for little pay. Only God could find that person.

I looked down at the assignment sheets in my hand. They took a lot of time each week but were necessary for clear communication with students and their parents, who would ensure the assignments were completed.

Since the school included students with learning differences, I individualized the weekly assignment sheets, requiring every student to work on similar concepts or skills. In addition to listing the assignments due the following week, the sheets included notes to the parents. Communication had never felt more essential in teaching than with students I only saw twice weekly.

My assistant and her two children arrived right on time. Stephanie's gift of organization was precisely the help I needed. She and I worked so well together that it was as if she could read my mind. I valued her help more than I could express.

"Good morning! What can I get started on?" Stephanie never wasted time, and I admired her for that.

"Do you want to start with the Columbus Day folders? Then maybe put prices on the new store items? Oh, and Trey is still the lead in the math competition. Would you update the chart?"

"Sure thing!"

The day was off to a great start. Kids and parents arrived; before I knew it, we were in the middle of our class. Parents typically stayed for a while, then left for a short time to run errands, but they would be back early to enjoy the contest.

* * *

Stephanie's son, Trey, skimmed the daily schedule on the chalkboard, dropped his backpack onto the table, unzipped it, and pulled out a pencil and math study packet. Today's contest included a math bee and speed drills, and Trey planned to win.

"Mrs. H, I stayed up way too late reading *The Lion, The Witch, and the Wardrobe,*" he said. He had dark circles under his eyes. He yawned.

"Trey! Of all nights to stay up late! I hope you're awake for the contest!"

"Do you have any coffee?"

"How about some water instead?" I tossed him a bottle.

"Okay, I guess."

"I finished the book. You know how you told me about Jesus being the Son of God and how He sacrificed Himself for my sins?"

"Uh-huh." Trey and I had been meeting individually to motivate him to read more and hone his writing skills. He liked to read exciting books with smart kids as characters and write a review of each book. I'd recommended C.S. Lewis's *The Chronicles of Narnia*.

One day, out of the blue, he talked about Jesus.

"I figured something out, Mrs. Huey."

"Oh, yeah? What?"

"Well, Aslan is like Jesus. I mean, Aslan didn't have to die. He did it on purpose. Died, I mean. "

"You're right. Amazing, isn't it?"

After the language arts block that morning, we took a break. All the kids knew the math contest would start just after the break.

First, the kids took their timed tests. Immediately, Stephanie scored them. Next, they divided into two groups for a math bee. The bee was down to Trey and one team member on one side of the room and Logan and one team member on the other side of the room. Both team members missed a fact, so Trey and Logan were at a standoff. The tension in the classroom was palpable. Trey seemed tired and nervous, and his confidence lagged. Ever confident, Logan won first place, with Trey a close second.

Trey stood speechless, his face red. I realized he was about to cry, and sure enough, he raced out of the classroom, leaving parents and students feeling awkward.

I looked at Stephanie, and she nodded. I left the students with her and the parents and followed Trey. I found him under the apple tree in the field.

"You're disappointed."

"Well, I hope you're not going to tell me I did a great job and my studying paid off because it didn't. I lost." For a ten-year-old, he thought like a teenager, probably because he had an older brother.

"Is there a better person to lose to than Logan? He works hard, too, you know."

"I know, but I wanted to win first place, Mrs. H. I worked so hard! And I told my dad I was going to win, so he said we were going dirt bike riding this weekend to celebrate. Now I have to tell him I lost!" He swiped at a renegade tear.

"You didn't exactly lose, Trey. You came in second place. And you tied with Logan for first place on the timed test."

"But I didn't win first place!"

"So, what would you have learned if you'd won first place?" I asked.

"Working hard pays off, but it sure didn't pay off for me."

"I wonder if God is showing you something." I sat down under the tree with him. We gazed at the valley below. "I wonder if he's speaking to your heart," I continued.

"Who cares?" His shrug fumed.

"I think you do, Trey. You said you saw a spiritual connection in the C.S. Lewis book. One of the main themes in Narnia is good versus evil. Hey, you said you prayed about winning. Do you remember the quote, 'He isn't safe, but he's good?'"

"Yeah, the Beaver said it. After that, he said, 'He's the King.'"

Well, I wonder if you could trust a good King? Our good God is trustworthy. You came in second today after much hard work, so you might think God didn't help you much. But can you agree He's good? For now?"

"I can think about it, I guess."

"And do you think you could go congratulate Logan?"

Trey and I stood up from under the apple tree and walked toward the classroom. His sister was running toward us.

"Mrs. H, Mom wants to know if you'll print the certificates."

"Is everything going okay?" It was unlike Stephanie to forget anything, and the certificates were on her list. I was surprised she hadn't left a parent in charge of the students.

"Yes, maybe she forgot." She looked at Trey, "And Mom needs YOUR help!"

The kids took off to the classroom, and I headed to my office in the house to print the certificates for the math competition winners.

As they printed, I thought about the earlier conversation with Trey. The truth is, I knew how disappointed he was. Some of his other classes didn't come as easily as math did, and he wanted that win more than anyone else in the classroom.

I glanced at the Norman Rockwell print and wondered how "Miss Jonesy" would have handled the situation.

I walked back to the classroom with the certificates in hand.

The first thing I noticed when I walked into the classroom was how quiet it was. And there was a table set up with juice and cookies, and was that a cake?

"HAPPY BIRTHDAY, MRS. HUEY!" the children shouted.

I was so surprised that I almost missed the happy birthday greetings on the chalkboard. When the kids finished singing an off-key Happy Birthday, instead of staying seated as in the Norman Rockwell painting, they ran up to give hugs. I laughed.

"HOW DID YOU KNOW IT WAS MY BIRTHDAY?" I couldn't help but ask.

"Mrs. Peggy knew. She planned the whole thing!"

The surprise party, I believe, was one of the best birthdays I'd ever had.

Trey and Logan enjoyed the party, wolfed down chocolate cake, and laughed together.

Maybe Jonsey would have handled things the same way I did, after all.

I knew then that this school, this ministry, was a mission He was part of. I realized that God was strengthening my faith and professional attempts every bit as much as he was strengthening Trey's. He showed me that the real lessons in the little red schoolhouse were eternal. And much like C.S. Lewis's Chronicles of Narnia, there were two realms—the physical and the spiritual. The two could not be separated.

I walked over and joined the parents at the party.

CHAPTER 7

A Teacher for
the 21ˢᵗ Century

"The future belongs to those who believe in the beauty of their dreams."

—ELEANOR ROOSEVELT

THE SCHOOL WAS in its seventh year, and I knew I needed to add a teacher or two, but I didn't realize it was so obvious until a conversation with Kathy, a parent.

"You really need help now, don't you?" Kathy was a parent who noticed things and said what was on her mind. Her four students were enrolled in the learning center, and she supported the academic inclusion model since one of her sons struggled in some areas, and her other children excelled. Our school worked beautifully for all of her kids, so she didn't need to enroll them into a couple of different schools.

"I've been praying about a science and math teacher. But the right person hasn't shown up, yet." I sighed.

Kathy and I walked to the classroom, enjoying the late spring afternoon. The sun struggled to peek out from behind clouds, but the unseasonably warm day made up for it. I was looking forward to a nice break soon since the school year was drawing to a close, but I was concerned about September's schedule. I did need a committed math and science teacher at the high school level, but one who could also connect with the younger students.

"My nephew just got married. His wife, Amorah, has a degree in science. I'm sure she could teach some math, too. Want her number?"

I called Amorah that afternoon, and she agreed to meet.

* * *

I could hardly hear the knock on the door due to our dachshund, Bogart, barking his head off and lunging viciously at it. I made a mental note to figure out how to break him from that when I had the time.

A beautiful young woman dressed casually stood at the door. Amazed she could smile under heavy attack from my miniature dachshund, I lunged for him and missed.

I ran around, feeling foolish, trying to sequester the dog while Amorah stood patiently, seemingly amused by the commotion.

Her unruffled demeanor impressed me, and I invited her in amid growling and barking and my unsuccessful efforts to curtail the chaos. Amorah did not attempt to shake off the dog, who, by now, had clamped his teeth on the hem of her jeans, shaking with all his might.

I cast a horrified glance at her during the kerfuffle. She looked down calmly and asked, "What is he doing?"

"He's protecting me. You are under attack, but I'll save you." I grabbed the raging dachshund and tossed him into his crate, where he promptly buried himself under his blanket and growled occasionally to let us know he was still in control.

Amorah would probably be able to handle most student issues if she could maintain her composure in this situation. I glared at Bogart, who growled again from his crate.

"Please sit down! Would you like some tea?"

"Maybe a little water?"

"Sure." I was feeling hot and noticed I was perspiring. *An auspicious beginning*, I thought wryly. I hoped to calm down in the kitchen.

I took our water glasses and sat across from her. Okay! So officially, I'm Patty Huey, and you're Amorah Nelson. So nice to meet you. Kathy said you were just married. Congratulations."

"Thank you!"

"As Kathy might have mentioned, I am looking for someone to teach science and math. You graduated from Seattle Pacific University, right?"

"Yes, I did. Now I'm finishing my Master's Degree in biology. I just have to defend my thesis. I will be very glad to get that behind me. I'm actually a little nervous about it!"

"I bet you'll be fine! Have you had any experience in instruction?"

"Yes, a little. I assisted my professor in working with his lab students and graded coursework. I guess you could call me an adjunct professor."

This was sounding really good. "That's great! How are you with teenagers?"

"I like kids. I have three younger brothers and a sister."

"Are you a Christian?"

"Yes."

"Would you be willing to teach Creation but also present the theory of evolution? I want the kids to see Truth for themselves. I think it's better to train kids how to think rather than tell them what to think. It helps them to better see how Creation trumps evolution theories."

Amorah thought for a minute. "Yes, I can do that with the right curriculum. Would you explain how the school works in detail? Kathy tried, but it was hard for me to understand. I was always in a five-day school, except for a brief time homeschooling, and this school is different."

"I know your academic experience has mostly been in five-day public school, so I understand it's a little hard to grasp the concept initially. Homeschoolers run the gamut from free-spirited unschooling to intellectual and academic pursuits. Some finish school by noon, while others work all day five days a week, strictly adhering to a schedule."

"Unschooling? What do you do with the unschoolers? How do they get credit?"

"That's the tricky part." We come alongside them, praising their efforts while encouraging their commitment to conform to our program. And you can't do that without a relationship.

"What do you mean?"

"If you take the time to get to know each parent and student and understand their struggles, that's a step in the right direction."

Again, Amorah thought for a minute.

She seemed to think before reacting, like the scientist that she was. Some people quickly speak their minds, but Amorah took her time. Her scientific mind reacted after analysis, and I appreciated her deliberateness. I would be surprised if she ever flew off the handle.

"There must be a lot of different struggles here. Of course, any student faces some struggle."

"For sure. Imagine teaching at home when you have five kids of all different ages and abilities. Now picture having a child with great potential and motivation and a developmentally disabled child at the same kitchen table."

"Seems almost impossible. Why do they do it?"

"I believe the parents in our school are called to it. They are willing to make the sacrifice. A one-income family is not prevalent in our society. Being in our school demands careful financial decisions."

Talking to Amorah felt easy. She appeared to be sincerely interested in my out-of-the-box learning center.

"You won't make much money to start. Just to let you know, I don't make a lot, either." I shrugged.

"That's okay. Whatever I make is more than I'm making now."

Again, that matter-of-fact honesty spoke to me.

"School starts in September. Does it sound like something you'd like to try?"

"Yes, I think so."

"Great! We'll meet again. I'm sure you'll have more questions after you think things through. We could meet a few times if you'd like. We'll need to talk about scheduling, curriculum, grading, coursework, etc. Would you like to see the classroom? That's where you'll be teaching."

That day, Amorah and I talked more, and I thought she would benefit the school and me.

How could I have known that in the future, Amorah and I would weather fierce storms together as we built the school's structure upon the foundation I'd begun? How could I have known then that she would take the school farther into the 21st century than I could and that she would face unimaginable obstacles?

After she drove away that day, I wondered what my chances were of coincidentally finding out from a parent about a young woman scientist interested in teaching at an out-of-the-ordinary learning center.

The answer was that it was no coincidence.

By the third time Amorah came to my house, Bogart greeted her with anticipation, just like I did.

CHAPTER 8

The Heart of the Matter

*"No matter what you do each day...or in life...doing
things God's way is a matter of the heart."*

—ELIZABETH GEORGE

I WAS USUALLY sitting at my computer working when the phone calls came.

"Hello, Hill Creek Christian."

"Hi, I'm calling to inquire about Hill Creek. I have a fifth-grade son, and we need a change."

"I'm happy to help you! Can you tell me a little about your son? Where is he currently attending school? Are there struggles?"

"Thomas is struggling a little, but I don't think it's because he can't learn. He doesn't seem to fit in his school or his class. He doesn't get the help he needs. When he gets home, he can't always tell me where he needs help, and I can't communicate well with his teacher. He seems depressed, and I'm worried."

"Would you like to meet to discuss things? If you agree, please bring your son so I can talk to him."

Typically, the parent was ready to meet that very day.

Or a conversation might go like this:

"Hello, I was referred to you by my friend. Our daughter is behind in school because she has a medical problem. Her blood sugars wake her up at night, and often, she's drained the next day and unable to focus. She's capable but usually needs more time to complete her assignments. Does Hill Creek offer any accommodations?"

Another went like this:

"We recently decided to homeschool, and our kids are doing fine, but they are complaining they need more competition. They miss having other kids in the classroom. My husband and I both graduated from UW, so our kids aspire to attend there, and we need an official transcript."

Other parents called for academic help with their son or daughter or both. Often, the homeschooling mom had young children as well as school-aged children at home. In every case, I realized that most families wanted a place to belong. They needed a place to feel accepted, a place to be encouraged, a Christian school with high morals and high academic standards that met their child's individual needs.

Back when I was in school, it didn't matter who you were, what family you came from, whether academics were easy or hard, and whether or not your family was well off. Everyone in our community attended the same local public school. All the teachers and most students went to church, too. Why? It was our culture then. We went to Sunday school and church. We went to church on Wednesday nights for fellowship and prayer, and we enjoyed outings with our church friends. Church filled two needs: spiritual and social. In those days, the local school did the same, and I thrived despite a rocky early childhood due to my biological parents' alcoholism. Once I moved to Alabama and was adopted by my aunt and uncle, I began to thrive.

From first grade through eighth grade, I went to the same elementary and middle school, and then my classmates and I were promoted to high school. I loved my school because it gave me stability. I knew the teachers, and they knew me. They sincerely cared about whether I thrived or not. I didn't get away with sloppy work because I knew the expectations. My new parents expected a lot from me, and I knew I needed to achieve. I loved the various challenges in the classroom such as math competitions, creative writing contests, citizenship speech writing and competition, California Achievement testing, auditions and drama, Bible day and passage memorization, not to mention fall festivals, the classroom Christmas parties, Valentine's Day parties, honor roll luncheons, and field trips. I loved it all because I belonged.

To sum up my school experience, I fit. And my parents did, too. They took pride in our school, participated often, and supported the teachers.

If it worked in the 1960s, why couldn't it work now? So, I transferred my personal school experience to Hill Creek, duplicating the model of the school my friends and I had attended. However, I also kept the one-room school model in mind, realizing the distinct similarities.

I was talking to a good friend out on my deck one day before school started in September. I'll never forget the conversation.

"I noticed your motto is a place where all students succeed. How can you honestly say that? You are an idealist who thinks that all kids will succeed."

"Well, I think they can if they feel secure, if all kids are visible, if there is good leadership from both the family and the school, if we recognize areas of deficit and monitor progress, and if we have high expectations. It takes work, but all kids can be successful."

"But there are always those kids who fail," she argued.

After she left that day, I wondered. Does God set people up for failure? I didn't think so.

If there is a secret to Hill Creek, a formula, it's that we try to create a place for everyone to belong. It's hard work for those who are called, but that's the heart of the matter.

CHAPTER 9

A Proven Hypothesis: The First Science Fair

"In questions of science, the authority of a thousand is not worth the humble reasoning of a single individual."

—GALILEO GALILEI

IT WAS THURSDAY after a long school day. Amorah and I had time to talk, plan school events, and relax-- a rarity. We had been working together for a while, and her classes were going well. I so appreciated the camaraderie.

As we discussed students who struggled with the workload, Amorah was particularly concerned about one of her high school students.

"He's failing the class because he won't do the work. I've tried everything. He doesn't even seem interested in the labs, and most kids love that part of my class. His parents are at their wit's end."

"I feel your frustration, Amorah. I'm probably pointing out the obvious, but sometimes, certain kids need us to believe in them when they can't see beyond their struggles. It's easy for them to get discouraged and quit trying. I believe that's what Chase is dealing with."

"I don't want him to fail my class."

"How much time do you have in your schedule? Maybe you could contact his mother and offer some tutoring. I'm sure she would leap at the opportunity."

"I'll give it a try."

"Let's go to the house where it's a little more comfortable!"

We walked from the classroom into the house. The fall leaves reminded me of confetti. It flashed through my mind that learners are much like the variations in those leaves. Some are more vibrant than others but fall like confetti at the slightest disturbance. Some leaves cling. Some drift. I had been pondering a way to reach kids not well-rooted in academics. Tutoring helped, but it didn't get to the root of the problem.

Amorah and I walked inside. I made a mental note to encourage her more often. But time was ever my enemy, and I battled it daily.

We discussed a few other challenges. One disgruntled parent had been complaining to others about the rigor of the English and science classes, and others had joined the protest. We needed to figure out a solution before this snowball became an avalanche.

"As long as we're available to help each student as much as possible, I don't think we need to alter our goals. We can always modify assignments if necessary. I think the biggest problem is that while homeschooling parents' hearts are in the right place, they struggle with time management. And, of course, they can't know every subject well. That's why they're here! Parents know their children better than teachers, but sometimes they struggle with presenting the material. By joining our efforts, kids get a well-rounded education—the best of both worlds.

"Could be." Amorah was thoughtful. "It's just uncomfortable knowing some parents disagree with us."

"I know. I dislike it, too."

"Patty, I want to tell you something. I have never really had anything bad happen to me."

I looked at young Amorah. Smart. Reliable. Honest. My heart melted. I thought about the circumstances in my life, and I knew that Amorah would face adversity in her life, and most definitely in teaching. Anytime we're doing God's work, we face difficulties. But I told myself not to focus on that with her right then.

I said instead, "Well, Christian school teaching is more challenging than my other jobs combined. God has taken me through extreme circumstances to prepare me for the next assignment. He's preparing you for something, too! And we're here to help each other!"

Amorah smiled.

"Hey. I have assigned my elementary, middle, and high school kids a science topic they will research and present to parents. Could you help me with it?"

"Sure!" Her face lit up. How I loved her willingness!

"What do you think about the elementary students presenting here in the classroom? My theory is that highlighting students' achievements is a great way for parents to feel a part of our academic goals. I have rented space at Hillcrest Lodge for the other students. There's a kitchen and plenty of tables and chairs. We could set up the displays and assign everyone a designated time to present projects."

"Sounds like a science fair to me." Amorah looked enthused.

"Yes, I guess it is. I'm more interested in the kids learning to write research papers. So, my focus is writing, but I thought a science topic would be good."

"Sounds like fun, Patty!"

I was amazed at her reaction, knowing this project would take even more of her time. "I'm not sure the kids think so. They're already nervous!" I smiled.

"How can I help?"

"It would be great if you could come to the elementary presentation and give me feedback—a critique of the science aspect. The bottom line is that I want to see the kids do more science. Linking English classes to a science topic seems like a good start.

* * *

To my delight, the elementary students were abuzz with excitement over presenting their projects. A refreshment table was ready for after the event. The kids and I tidied up the classroom and set up their colorful projects. The topics included butterflies, eagles, volcanoes, rocks and minerals, sprouting seeds, growing crystals, and soap making.

Before we knew it, parents, relatives, and Amorah had arrived to hear the presentations. I quickly reminded the students that they were the experts on their topics due to their in-depth research. As they began their presentations, confidence trumped anxiety. At the end of the program, the parents applauded.

Amorah had critiqued the displays as planned, and I was looking forward to her feedback.

On cue, Amorah walked to the front of the classroom and said, "Your projects look great! Your presentations were thorough, and you informed your audience. Your boards are neat and organized." Several of the parents nodded.

"I have a question, though. Would you like to do this again in a slightly different way? Scientists start with a question when researching. It's called a hypothesis. Maybe next year, you could present your question and answer it through your research."

The students, proud of their most recent science achievement, seemed excited. Parents nodded.

After everyone was gone and Amorah and I were alone, I asked for more feedback.

"Well, everyone was prepared!" she said.

"Yes, I thought so, too. Their research papers were well-written after many edits."

"Are your high school English students presenting similarly?" she asked.

"Yes, why?"

"If you agree, I'd like to see them complete an actual science fair project with a panel of judges. Learning the scientific method will prepare the kids who are going to college. And even if they aren't, it's suitable for learning logic."

A few days later, we were at Hillcrest Park Lodge with 175 parents and students. We had decided on a potluck since the projects would run through the dinner hour. I was mortified to see there was not enough food! Those at the end of the line would have a light dinner to be sure! I made a mental note to assign food at the next event. Even so, the parents were laughing and having a great time getting to know each other better.

The amount of effort put into the projects was impressive. Parents were pleased with their students' demonstrations, as were the others. Amorah's student, Chase, had enthusiastically participated, and I hoped his success would ignite future motivation. The camaraderie between students and parents showed. Any frustration over the difficulty level of the science and English classes seemed resolved for now. Thank you, God!

Amorah and I ended the event by passing out ribbons. Parents applauded their students. They stayed afterward and put away the tables and chairs, enjoying their time together.

By the end of the evening, Amorah was energized. "Next year

will be much better!"

"Better?" I asked.

"Yes, we'll have an actual science fair!" Amorah talked as we packed up. "I'll start early in the year and show them examples. Maybe they can choose their topics, or I'll assign them."

I added, "We could offer prizes for first, second, and third-place winners."

"Sounds good to me! How about we add medals?"

And just like that, our annual science fair was born.

I hadn't known it then, but Amorah and I had modeled the scientific process between us. We hypothesized that highlighting students' work efforts and achievements would be a way to develop parent cohesiveness. During meetings with Amorah, we predicted the outcomes of what a presentation might accomplish. The data we used were the projects and combined effort of parents, students, and the two of us. We analyzed the data throughout the six weeks of work on the projects with everyone involved. We concluded that the issue with parents thinking our classes were too academic was resolved through school cohesiveness sealed by a joint project.

I observed that parents had been entirely involved in their students' projects. They now knew the work was not too difficult. They saw their students' potential first-hand and saw their confidence soar. I prayed that next year's science fair would continue to benefit the school's overall spirit.

As I drove away from Hillcrest Lodge that evening, I thought about how Hill Creek was an experiment. Could Hill Creek be a place where all students succeed? After all, we had made progress with Chase and a few others.

I imagined that the school would continue to change lives one student at a time and continue well into the 21st Century. It would take much prayer. Humans tend to wear out.

I know because I only wanted to get home, have a cup of tea, and relax.

CHAPTER 10

A New Look

"God never said that the journey would be easy,
but He did say that the arrival would be worthwhile"

–Max Lucado

AMORAH AND I managed to share the classroom for a period of time, but it wasn't easy. Eventually, juggling classes in the red schoolhouse became challenging. With two days a week for high school, one for elementary, and one for middle school, our driveway resembled a bustling highway. Fortunately, our neighbor behind us lived a few acres away in her house on the hill, and her horses grazed behind a fence just across from our road. Our other neighbors were about an acre away on one side and about three acres away on the other. Still, I endured stares here and there when I was outside or walking to the mailbox, about a quarter mile away.

I knew we had to make some changes. The first simple change I made was to hire a cleaning lady. Since there was no restroom in the classroom, everyone used our downstairs bathroom and, on occasion, the one upstairs. Two parents helped organize the classroom and monitored the kids as they walked from the classroom to the house. I appreciated them keeping things orderly.

Steve, who had been more than supportive of the school, now said he was considering renting a place to live. I'm still not sure whether or not he was kidding. I thought it best not to ask.

Amorah and I discussed it and agreed we needed more space. But where?

For years now, I'd been walking on the dike that ran behind the pond in front of our house. Our neighbors, the Van Polens, had graciously invited me to walk anytime across their covered bridge to the dike. I made the walk at least once a day—twice if I could. I could get a couple of miles in if I walked from our house, across the bridge, and down the dike and back. It was plenty of time to clear my head and relax. Much like those laps on the track from long ago, the dike walks were times well spent with God and nature. When I walked, I prayed. He often spoke through my thoughts. I thanked him for the day's victories. I asked for wisdom in dealing with struggles. And He always gave me insight, but most of all, He gave me peace.

On the dike walk, I traversed along the edge of nature. The creek ran north and south and was full of wildlife. When I saw a deer, I was reminded of the verse from the Psalms, "As the deer pants for water, my soul longs for thee." On other days, I watched eagles and was reminded of Isaiah 40: "Those who wait for the Lord shall renew their strength." Tolerant beavers shared the creek with swans and ducks. That walk was the closest thing to Paradise I'd ever experienced and likely ever will on Earth.

One such day, I had walked the dike during an unexpected lull. The dogs and I dashed out the door, the three of us delighted with this unexpected gift. They bolted across the bridge and over the creek, where they swam, dug, and chased a duck or two. I meandered behind.

"God, it's me again." Immediately, I felt His presence.

"We have to do something about all the kids. Did you hear that our neighbors think we're running a drug ring? I think it's all the cars."

A thought occurred. *Don't worry about what people think.*

"We're stacked in like sardines. I don't know what to do. The little store I've had my eyes on in Conway has been rented. I've looked around at other rentals. Nothing seems to be available or suitable."

One of the dogs barked at me. I hadn't realized it, but I had stopped just outside the covered bridge, and he probably thought I was talking to myself.

"Lord, what will we do if you don't intervene?"

As they often did, an eagle flew overhead to a fir tree. But today, the flight caught my attention.

Another thought came to mind. *Wait.*

I prayed about a few other things and completed the rest of the walk. I hurried to my next appointment.

Back at the house, I put the dogs up and raced back to the classroom just in time for a mom to drive up for a scheduled conference. Conferences were a time for parents and me to get to know each other. As they began to trust me, I learned how to assist them.

Tracy and I had just finished the conference when she mentioned that her son had said that the classroom was getting crowded.

I explained to her that I had been looking for space.

"Would you like me to talk to Reverend Blair, my pastor? I'm sure he would allow the school to meet at our church. It has several classrooms and a chapel."

Tracy's church was an older church in a small town about twelve miles away.

From deep inside, I felt a nudge.

Trust.

"Sure, Tracy, if you don't mind. We have forty-eight kids, and when parents attend the various events, we might have close to two hundred in attendance."

She looked thoughtful. "The chapel could easily accommodate that many. "

A couple of days later, Tracy carpooled kids to school. She walked briskly into the classroom.

"Got a minute?"

"Of course."

"Would you be available to tour the church tomorrow afternoon? Pastor Blair thinks Hill Creek would be a good fit for the church."

"Absolutely!"

The next day, I drove into the spacious church parking lot.

Tracy was there waiting. Once inside, she introduced me to Reverend Blair, who appeared reserved but kind.

The classrooms were color-coded, and an idea for a color-coded schedule popped into my mind. The open kitchen connected to a spacious fellowship hall complete with a stage. The church was not huge, but it was not small, either. A perfect fit for our school. It was centrally located for those driving from the south and the north. But worry invaded the joy of the moment. What if the folks driving from Mount Vernon in the Skagit Valley felt the travel time was too far, especially since the school had practically been at their back door?

It's only a couple of days a week for each grade level.

Over the next few days, Reverend Blair created a rental contract. HCC would officially kick off the new school year in a building other than the little red schoolhouse. I knew it was a good move, but I felt wistful.

In late spring, Amorah and I made the announcement to the parents. Some were excited, but as expected, some lamented leaving the red schoolhouse. And that set me to thinking during a few sleep-less nights.

Amorah and I needed to talk.

After class one day, Amorah and I discussed how to manage our new space. "Why not have two campuses?" she asked.

I had been thinking that very thing. "Great idea!"

We agreed that the high school would meet in Stanwood, and the elementary and middle school would continue in the red schoolhouse.

On my walk the next day, I asked God what He thought.

A thought flashed into my mind. *Why not ask the students?*

We did, and the students and parents seemed pleased with the plan.

* * *

When Steve got home from work that same day, we sat on the porch enjoying a cup of coffee while watching an eagle soar above.

"Guess what?" I asked.

"What?"

"The church in Stanwood is a go! That means fewer kids here next year."

We high-fived, but he was unexpectedly quiet.

"What does "fewer" mean?"

I explained the new model, and he grinned. "I like having some kids here. Keeps things alive."

"They sure do!"

"Hey! Let's celebrate! Want to go to Anthony's for dinner?"

"You bet!" I jumped up to get ready.

Steve was already making the reservation.

CHAPTER 11

Lynn Raises the Bar

"…but there is a friend who sticks closer than a brother."

—Proverbs 18:24

AS TIME PASSED and HCC's foundation cemented, we saw a need for another teacher. One person at the top of our list was a friend who'd run her own learning center in Seattle for a few years but had recently moved from Seattle to Arlington. I wondered if she'd join us now that she was closer.

Lynn and I had met several years before at an Academy Northwest teacher's meeting. She was a Christian, a true intellectual, and an energetic teacher who believed in challenging her students. Lynn was not afraid to tackle complex projects. And she possessed a valuable trait—wisdom. Adversity is a good teacher, and Lynn had experienced her fair share of adversity, having been widowed at thirty-nine. She was still in the process of raising and homeschooling her four children. While a couple of her kids had attended the prestigious Lakeside School in Seattle, she noticed that the spiritual aspect was missing, so she decided to homeschool instead.

Early in our friendship, we'd thought of starting a school together. The program would emphasize our nation's Christian heritage, where patriotism was encouraged, and where an in-depth study of the Constitution was mandatory. Even then, we realized that revisionist history was being taught, and we knew the results would prove disastrous. We entertained the idea of fighting the culture and doing our best to preserve our nation's heritage. But, at the time, Lynn had been quite involved in her successful Seattle learning center, and I was deeply entrenched in HCC; thus, our idea of a Patrick Henry College-type prep school never manifested.

Now that Lynn had settled into her new life in Arlington, I asked her to join Hill Creek for a couple of reasons. We needed another English class; if she accepted, she would teach honors English. Secondly, I was experiencing some challenging family issues. My father was gravely ill, and trying to run the school and transport him to dialysis three times per week, in addition to helping my mother, proved exhausting. Additionally, Justin, who had graduated from high school, required assistance transitioning into the workforce and the demands of adulthood.

So, I asked Lynn if she would consider joining us. She said she'd pray about it, and after a few days, she accepted. I was elated! It was an understatement to say HCC was fortunate to have her on board.

Lynn spent hours prepping for her honors English class. Initially, her students were shocked at the high standards, but each of them adjusted and rose to her level of expectations. Lynn was a no-nonsense teacher who did not accept excuses for missed assignments or tardiness in her honors English class. Her in-depth assignments not only taught students how to write, but they taught them how to think critically. Soon, a healthy competition ignited in her classroom as students eagerly strove for first place. The first-place student would be honored at the awards night at the end of the school year. A first-place win could be written into college scholarship letters, assisting the student in landing significant funds for college.

She and I enjoyed working together and especially planning the writers' conferences. Each year, we had a new theme. Topics included poetry, short stories, screenplays, and novelettes. The work was intense, but we found great satisfaction in the annual events.

One day, Lynn told me, "Patty, you treat every student as though he has potential learning challenges." She was not being critical but straightforward. My first reaction was to disagree. After all, Hill Creek was a school where students with learning challenges were included! And I made modifications where needed. Her comment made me think. I had a long history of friendship with Lynn—a friendship built on honesty. I valued her insight and wisdom. She also had a laser-sharp eye that sliced away at the core of things. I needed to think. To pray. I needed to examine my motives. My philosophy.

As I did, a few things surfaced. One of my significant insecurities was that I'd only raised one child, and he had disabilities. As a homeschool teacher, did I have adequate experience to assist homeschooling parents in educating their typical kids? Most parents I worked with were efficient, organized, and focused, with clear goals in mind. I had the same mindset and abilities, but my son and I had a different situation. Did that matter? I was afraid it did. Was I viewing all students through the lens of my own son's struggles? I'd taught for over twenty years. I did have experience with a variety of learners. Still, Lynn had seen "something" that sparked the comment! I had to check myself.

Lynn had asked a good question. I wondered if I was trying to "fix" students even if they didn't need fixing! Fixing and educating were two separate goals. I spent many sleepless nights tossing my thoughts around. *Help me see what I need to see, Lord.*

Day after day, I prayed about this. All types of learners could function in the same classroom if assignments were modified and student issues were accommodated. Of course, I couldn't expect all students to perform at the same level. Was I elevating the students with disabilities? Focusing mainly on them while lowering the standards of regular and above-average students? If so, I was touting a faulty inclusion model, and I'd have to keep a close eye on myself, which I did, thanks to Lynn's question.

I was reminded that HCC was, of course, focusing on preparing all students academically, but it was also focused on presenting them with tools for learning, tools to manage and organize themselves, and tools to strengthen their spiritual lives. In other words, we were preparing the students to take charge of their own learning—to be independent learners.

Sometimes it takes another person to point out things we can't see for ourselves. When I look back, Lynn's tenure at HCC was paramount in raising the academic bar at the school. Leave it to Lynn to notice that our inclusion model needed to be tweaked.

A couple of years later, Lynn enrolled her son, Mark, in a Current Issues class I was teaching. There were thirteen high school students in the class, three of whom had learning challenges. I had no trouble adjusting assignment sheets and making the necessary accommodations for all students, including above-average learners like Mark. The class allowed each student to achieve his or her full potential. Lynn told me later that she'd recommend Current Issues to other parents because she appreciated the high standards for her son.

Years later, Lynn and I stay in touch regularly. We have emailed frequently for many years. All these years later, Lynn continues to encourage me and challenge me to think critically while holding me accountable in several aspects of my life, with my writing goals being one of those aspects.

Lynn left her indelible mark upon Hill Creek, for which I am extremely grateful.

CHAPTER 12

A Christian Writers' Conference

"The worst part of holding the memories is not the pain.
It's the loneliness of it. Memories need to be shared."

–LOIS LOWRY

I NOTICED A pattern with my students in English and writing classes. Some of the top students were not as creative as students who struggled, yet some of those who struggled had little motivation to write other than to earn a decent grade. I scheduled a field trip to the Young Author's conference, hoping it might put a little pizzazz into the students' writing.

The day arrived for the field trip. The excited kids, equipped with notebooks and pencils, looked forward to a day out of the classroom. We checked in at the local community college where the conference was held. First, we listened to the keynote author's address and then attended breakout writing workshops throughout the day. I was slightly perturbed that some presenters used language I didn't approve of, and the shared story selections didn't appear appropriate for the students' ages. In fact, I didn't think they were appropriate for any age, but I tried to ignore it.

The students enthusiastically participated in the various workshops. That year, the overall focus was on short story writing. The students were asked to bring a short story they had written in their classrooms from prompts that Young Authors had previously assigned. The students and I worked hard on their individual stories, and they were ready to share.

At the end of the day, the keynote author asked volunteers to read their short story selections. I was shocked to hear that many story themes dealt with murder, the occult, sorcery, and scenes of a lascivious nature! While I didn't want any fourth, fifth, and sixth graders subjected to those topics, I certainly wanted HCC students steered away from them. It was too late for that year, but I vowed to change things the following year.

At the end of the conference, I spoke with a presenter who was busy packing his books and other items. He looked up and smiled.

"Your conference was well organized. Thank you for all your hard work."

"Yes, some good things happened today! A few kids seem spurred on to write. They certainly shared some great stories!" He continued to pack his belongings.

"I agree that the kids were excited to hear a fresh approach, and some of the stories were compelling. But in the future, I would like better guidelines regarding what is and is not appropriate to write about."

"In other words, do you want to censor their writing?" the presenter looked offended as he shoved his books and other items into a case.

"I didn't like the swearing, and some of the story topics were dark. The classroom teachers would willingly follow carefully thought-out guidelines for this age group." I hoped I didn't sound judgmental. I just wanted him to consider my viewpoint.

He zipped his case and said, "The kids know what they like to read, and they write similarly to what they read. They like to read what's trendy!"

I decided to let it go. "Okay. I just wanted you to know my perspective." I already knew what I was going to do.

Right away, I called Peggy King Anderson, a published author and friend who taught writers' workshops.

"I'd love to teach a workshop for your students!" Her joy and enthusiasm warmed me. She told me her ideas for the workshop, and I was so enthused I wanted her to speak to the children right away.

"How about next spring?" she asked. "I'm booked until then."

Next spring? Well, I'd get it scheduled, and next year, we'd have a Christian writers' conference! "That'll work just fine!"

I ended the phone call happy that Peggy did not mind driving the sixty miles from Bellevue. And her fee was minimal.

At our first conference the following spring, I watched as Peggy inspired a dozen students. Her natural exuberance and genuine love for children charmed them, and I was happy to see writing excitement abound.

Later, we held a small classroom competition, and the school year ended on a happy note. I knew then that we would hold a conference the next school year similar to the one we'd participated in at the community college. I started thinking early about inviting a published author. Maybe we'd include a contest. I'd have to ask for people to volunteer to judge the manuscripts. And I'd need a rubric. I sat down and started a list of things I'd need to get done before next year.

The second year, a former missionary and published author, Robert Elmer, spoke in an all-day writer's workshop. We had read one of Robert's mysteries, and the students loved it. Before the conference, we had worked for six weeks on short stories, and their completed manuscripts were turned in to the judges. I already knew the winners and was excited to announce them. That year, at the end of the conference, I realized I needed to include the high school group in the next writers' conference.

Those first two writers' conferences set the foundation for years to come. I learned I needed to start early praying for God to reveal what the next one would look like and who would speak. Sometimes, we were right down to the wire before God led us to the right person.

* * *

One year, our team chose memoir as the writers' conference genre. By now, we had explored several other genres, including short stories, novelettes, screenplay and creating trailers, poetry, journalism, and epics. The memoir genre scared me a little. I wasn't worried about researching it and teaching the kids, but I was worried about time. Both Amorah and I had heavy workloads, including leadership responsibilities, chapel oversight, teaching classes, teachers' meetings, and student-parent conferences.

How could I do justice to the genre? Quality was necessary, but so was the spiritual aspect. The summer before, I'd created a curriculum map for the year. I knew how much time I had, and worry set in. To complicate things, Steve, my mother, and I planned to go to Alabama for a one-hundredth celebration of the church I had attended growing up. As much as I was looking forward to it, I knew it would devour a chunk of my time.

"Lord," I prayed one day on the way home from school, "help me manage my time and help memoir writing honor You. Please give me some fresh new ideas." I drove into my driveway and felt a weight lift from my shoulders. A few days later, it occurred to me that

I could have someone help me teach the memoir writing, so I asked one of the pastor's daughters, a former homeschooler and teacher. She graciously accepted my request. Now I just needed to figure out a speaker for the conference. Every trail I pursued wound up a dead end. Time was running out.

The second semester came, and we headed to Alabama. It's hard to thoroughly enjoy a trip when something is hanging over your head. While I was there, I had to surrender to God to quell my anxiety. I needed to find a speaker, as there were only eleven weeks until the writers' conference.

Due to circumstances, I would fly on a separate flight from my family, so I was sitting at the Birmingham airport alone with one other passenger about an hour before our scheduled flight. I was grading papers.

"Are you a teacher?" He had a British accent rather than a Southern accent. People in Alabama talk to strangers, and asking questions is not considered rude.

I smiled. "Yes, I work at being one, anyway."

The man had a kind face. "Where I'm from, teachers are greatly respected. Where do you teach?"

"I teach in a small private school for homeschoolers in Mount Vernon, Washington."

"Oh! A long way from home, then! Tell me about your school." The man seemed sincerely interested. He settled into his seat. He was a medium-built man with ebony skin and a distinguished look. *Was he from England? No, the accent wasn't quite British.*

"As I said, it's a small school for homeschoolers. We meet a couple of days each week." I shrugged. "For a small school, it sure creates a lot of work. And worry." I was surprised I added something so personal. But there was something about him.

CHAPTER 13

What Makes Christian Homeschooling Different?

"In all your ways acknowledge Him, and He shall direct your paths."

–Proverbs 3:6

I LOOKED OVER the many varieties of apples at Safeway, wondering which would be best for a new dessert, when a former HCC parent tapped me on the shoulder. We dodged other shoppers as we caught up on our lives and families.

"Patty, Melody has thrived because of Hill Creek. That school was different because of the relationship you, Amorah, and her teachers developed. I think it's because you took the time to know what motivated her. Her worldview and her academics flourished. When other parents have asked me what made HCC different, I told them it was the relationship aspect."

I walked away from that conversation, encouraged to hear about Melody's life, but I also began to wonder what makes Christian schools different. And what about Hill Creek? What makes Hill Creek different?

The question continued to surface throughout the day, so that evening, I went upstairs to my office and viewed a PowerPoint Amorah and I had created. Hill Creek's motto is "To know Christ and make Him known through Christian education." I wondered how many HCC students knew Jesus and had made Him known to others in and out of school.

As I viewed the PowerPoint slides, it hit me that any Christian school could make a similar claim. So how, I wondered, is HCC different? How is it genuinely Christian?

Looking at various Christian school websites, the casual observer might notice that most parents desire a solid academic foundation for their children. Almost every parent wants a well-educated child, and all parents want a safe place for their children to learn and make friends.

For many years in the United States, public and Christian schools looked quite similar. They set similar standards, held to similar morals and values, and, overall, had the same goals for their enrolled students. Even secular curricula reflected biblical truth. As previously mentioned, I had attended a public school in Alabama where we prayed each morning and enjoyed Bible Day each Thursday. Christian parents sent their children to public school knowing that the school administration and teachers adhered to a common faith and family values.

Sadly, over time, things have changed. Today, the worldview of public schools is distinctly secular. It's common knowledge that prayer was removed years ago. I wonder how many parents realize that revisionist history is currently being taught. That capitalism, a distinctive of American life, is undermined while socialism is highlighted. That the theory of evolution is taught as fact with no thought of presenting Creation. That health classes are conducted with a distorted focus.

Of course, there are a few exceptions. A friend who recently moved from the West Coast now works in a public school where Bible verses are displayed in classrooms. Many teachers there are Christian, but that is no longer the norm for most public schools.

The difference between Christian and public schools lies in something other than academics. The subjects offered in public schools often exceed those in a small Christian school. Any parent would notice that right away.

To fully arrive at an answer, I needed to examine the core of each school's purpose. A school's soul or heart needed to be more than a mission statement. More than doctrinal beliefs. More than academics.

As I delved further into the differences, I observed that the public school's worldview is more than secular. That worldview focuses on current trends and particular types of instruction to ensure specific student outcomes.

So, what is wrong with that method? Students do need to be prepared for the future. I arrived at an answer I already knew to be true. The public school method is based on secular humanism, which leaves the God of the Bible out of the picture. The definition of secular humanism is evidence-based decision-making. Everything must be visible and testable.

Next, I looked at Hill Creek. At its heart, Hill Creek holds to a biblical worldview. We see God in the form of Jesus. At HCC, we explore education and life through a different lens. After all, the Bible is the primary source for studying historical and contemporary writers, philosophers, and theories.

I am writing this chapter well after the COVID-19 shutdown, but it's still fresh on my mind. Most people experienced several frustrations due to the pandemic. With churches shut down, many students at home meeting online for classes, few social outlets, vacations canceled, and new government mandates, depression has run rampant even in our Christian and secular children. So, which worldview do we use when addressing interpersonal struggles, including depression and suicide? How do we answer questions about what happens after we die or when a student asks where God is amid a pandemic? Do we use a Christian worldview or a secular worldview?

Feeling encouraged, I confirmed my thinking about how Christian school is different. But what about a school like Hill Creek, where students attend a private homeschool program? I thought about it and decided that even many public school students currently use a homeschool model, including online classes. Some have even been homeschooled, at least temporarily. They were forced into it due to COVID-19. So, what is the difference?

Hill Creek's homeschool Christian program is known for building relationships with the students and partnering with parents to strengthen each student's Christian walk and worldview.

As I write this, I am aware that the majority of parents today will choose a secular school over a Christian school. However, contemporary parents have a decision to make regarding their children's education. These parents must realize that their children's worldview will not primarily be developed by academics but by the influence of their teachers and their relationship with classmates. With HCC's enrollment currently at total capacity, it appears that many parents are reasoning that HCC's Christian offering of high academics and godly, personal relationships eclipse a secular worldview. I turned off my computer and walked downstairs.

"You've been quiet this evening," Steve said. "What's up?"

"Oh, I've just been doing a little thinking. Want some tea?"

"Sure."

As we sat with our steaming cups, I asked him, "So tell me about the teachers you remember. What made them stand out? Was it their teaching style or because they took time to get to know you?"

We talked for a long time that evening.

CHAPTER 14

The First Chapel

"Do what you can with all you have, wherever you are."

–THEODORE ROOSEVELT

"PATTY, CHAPEL STARTS in half an hour. You asked me to re-
mind you."

I looked up from the student I was working with. "Thanks, Rick.
I'll be right there. "

My student asked, "What do we do at chapel?"

"We'll sing, hear a short message, and pray. Like a short church
service."

One day, as I walked into the fellowship hall, a question popped
into my head. Why wouldn't a Christian school be holding regular
chapels? If we did, who would lead? What about the music? Who
would deliver the message? Well, I told myself, I'd think about it later.

But I couldn't shake the thought. I'd wake up in the night planning it. I started asking students if they were interested. I wondered
when to hold a chapel so most students could attend.

A music team would not be a problem. Hill Creek seemed to
attract talented students who could play an instrument and sing.

And there was Rick.

While teaching at a local parent partnership program in Mount Vernon, I met Rick's mom, Sally. She had voiced her unhappiness with the program there, so I told her about Hill Creek.

Her children caught my attention because both stood out from the rest. Rick was a natural leader, and his sister, Haley, had a gift for uniting students to a common cause. What a pair those two were! Rick, an eighth grader, was tall, blonde, and serious. His blue eyes seemed to pack a burden, and he appeared to have escaped early teenage immaturity. This boy was well beyond his years.

My experience told me he had seen adversity. I was drawn to him for that reason.

His sister, Haley, who was in sixth grade, presented as solid, mature, and focused. She was graceful, quiet, and shy. Both students stood out from the crowd. Rick had learned guitar and could sing, and another student was teaching Haley to play piano. I'd heard that she was learning quickly.

Their mom, an extrovert, was strict. Excuses were not tolerated, and her kids rose to her expectations.

Time passed, and my year at the parent partnership ended. The following year, Sally placed her children in Hill Creek, and I was delighted.

Rick and Haley set a high standard for their classmates.

It seemed right that Rick would serve as chaplain. I asked his mother about it, and she was okay with the idea as long as he could keep up his grades.

I scheduled a meeting with Rick.

"What do you think of adding a once-a-month all-school chapel? I thought we could include praise, worship, and a short message."

"You know, I had wondered about that myself. I think it would keep the kids focused spiritually and pull the school together, too. We could include announcements."

"That's true. I like the announcement idea. It would be a good way to keep kids motivated as we focus on upcoming activities." Rick was clearly on board.

"Who are you thinking for the lead? What about the music? I think Deborah, Rachel, and Haley," Rick suggested.

"I think the girls would be interested. Great choices! They can all sing and play piano, and you play guitar. Could you juggle being the lead chaplain and your academic workload? You have a heavy load this year."

"I thought you'd never ask!" He smiled. "I'd really like to, and I know I can keep my grades up. Chapel will only be once a month."

"Okay. Why don't we plan on next month? Maybe the first Tuesday of each month? I can email you some ideas I have about the structure. Take a look, and then we can talk again. Okay?"

Teachers feel positive energy in a school or classroom when things are going well. I noticed that energy as the students prepared for the first chapel. They talked about it in the hallway, posted signs announcing it, and made classroom announcements. I could see God's hand in this new endeavor.

But things of God often don't come easy.

At the end of class one day, Haley lingered. Patty, do you have a minute to talk?

Her eyes seemed dull.

"Sure."

She began to cry. Huge tears rolled down her cheeks. Sobs racked her body. I quickly closed the door and put my hand on her shoulder until she calmed down. "Come. Sit down. Tell me what's going on." I expected she had received a bad grade or had a bad day in class. Now, she had become even more of a perfectionist.

Finally, she was able to speak. "It's Mom and Dad and all the fighting. Last night they were talking about divorce."

Shock radiated through my body, and I fought to stay calm. Sally and Dave divorced? How could that be?

"Oh, no, I can imagine how upset you are! How can I help?"

"I don't know. They fight all the time. Rick and I usually stay in our rooms unless we're doing chores. If we get everything done, sometimes things are calmer. But not last night."

Interesting how God uses one person's circumstances to understand another's. My biological parents had also divorced, and I remembered the pain, confusion, and tension.

Haley and I talked things through. I let her know she could talk to me any time.

Later, Rick, who seemed subdued, met with me. His concern was the school. He was concerned they might need to leave. I assured him we'd do everything we could.

When Sally and Dave split up, she could no longer pay tuition. The other teachers, understandably devastated by Rick and Haley's situation, voted to waive tuition to offer the kids stability.

Haley had become best friends with some girls in one of the Hill Creek families. She often spent time at their home doing homework and eventually became part of that family.

Rick, a high schooler now, was striving for a 4.0 to get to college with little debt. The teachers encouraged him as best as they could. He took on the role his father had left behind by managing the household chores and helping his mom and sister. Rick had grown up fast. And I worried about that because when kids miss out on a part of their childhood, they often revert later.

God heard our prayers and provided distractions from family turmoil in the form of other students and their families who invited the kids into their homes. He also provided leadership roles within the school. Rick was always the one to set up for classes by moving chairs, making copies for teachers, emptying trash at the end of the day, and serving in the classroom as a teacher's assistant.

So, it seemed fitting that Rick would be the first Hill Creek chaplain.

As I walked to the chapel, I reminded a few loitering students that chapel was beginning and asked them to join us. Out of curiosity, they did.

When I walked into the chapel, I felt the Spirit move. I knew God was in our midst.

Rick welcomed everyone, and then he and the worship team led us in a couple of praise songs. One student sang a solo. The tone was set.

I looked at the students' faces, rapt with interest and expectation. They all knew Rick's struggle.

He walked to the podium and asked that everyone in the future bring a Bible to the chapel services. He asked those with Bibles to turn to 2 Corinthians 4: 8-9. Then he looked at his classmates with serious eyes and asked, "Have you experienced a burden lately? Maybe it's a friendship gone wrong, the pressure of school, or family problems. Maybe you're feeling like checking out. But be encouraged." And then he read from his Bible. "We are hard pressed on every side, but not crushed; perplexed, but not in despair; persecuted, but not abandoned, struck down, but not destroyed."

Rick spoke from his heart and ended with thanking the Lord. He reminded the students that God can change burdens into blessings. "All of you and this school are a blessing to me. Now, ask yourself how your burdens have become blessings."

Rick invited any struggling students to pray with him. He also told them he would happily talk with them anytime about their struggles. He encouraged them to come to the next chapel, where they would divide into groups for more intimate discussion.

I left that day with my spirit filled. Hill Creek's monthly chapel would be more than a time of spiritual focus. It would be a place where students could be real with each other, seeking support and sharing concerns. Through the first chapel, the school experienced God's power and direction. Again, I wondered what He would do next.

CHAPTER 15

Teaching for the 21st Century

"I play the notes as they are written,
but it is God who makes the music."

–J. S. BACH

MORE TEACHERS JOINED us, and enrollment increased. I liked to think of them as teachers for the 21st Century. I realized that we needed a strict standard for the subjects we were teaching. Academy Northwest followed state guidelines for graduation, of course, and we followed them. But did Hill Creek have its own Christian standards? I was teaching from a biblical worldview using Christian language arts and history curriculum, and I knew that Amorah was doing the same in science. We used other carefully examined materials to supplement the main curriculum but needed to ensure that new teachers held our same worldview. I wanted to do everything possible to lead students to the right path—the narrow path. For them to be on that path, they would need to hold firmly to their faith and learn to think critically about Christianity. After all, research, even then, was showing how post-high school young people were abandoning their faith at high rates. Did that have to happen? Could we make a difference here at our school?

As I write this chapter, we are approaching the 400th anniversary of the landing of our Pilgrim fathers. I have been scanning the news, hoping to see news articles proclaiming this foundational event. I finally found one article. While I was not entirely shocked, I did feel a deep sorrow. What had happened to contemporary America where teachers once taught about our nation's Christian heritage without apology and where critical thinking was emphasized?

Over the years, I have noticed that the story of the Pilgrims has not been taught in public schools or even in some Christian schools. In fact, I wonder how many elementary-age children across our nation have learned about our Pilgrim fathers. For example, when my family and I were stationed at Pearl Harbor in Hawaii, I planned lessons on the Pilgrims around the Thanksgiving holiday. My students there had no idea who the Pilgrims were. It is no secret that Thanksgiving and the Pilgrims' landing have been deemphasized. It is my opinion that it is an error in judgment not to highlight our nation's Christian heritage in the classroom. If we fail to do so, we weaken our society for future generations.

It's good for our students to know that from the Pilgrims came the Mayflower Compact, a document heavily influenced by the Bible, and that outlined civil affairs. This document was a precursor to our Constitution, which established the laws of our land from a Judeo-Christian worldview. Students who are taught the foundations of American history understand the importance of holding onto our godly heritage, our Constitution, and, ultimately, our freedoms. The enemies of our free-market system will not dupe those individuals.

Amorah and I discussed all this and the courses we offered. When we interviewed teachers, we expressed the importance of including our nation's heritage with a strong Christian emphasis. We conveyed that our classes, including math and world literature, should be taught from a biblical worldview. And we discussed the importance of teaching the students to think critically.

One day, a parent walked into my classroom at the end of the day.

"Mind if I talk to you for a few minutes?" Susan asked.

"Of course not! Have a seat."

"I'll get to the point. Your English and history classes almost seem like Bible classes. I didn't have to worry about this sort of thing when we were in public school." Susan, a mom I respected, appeared flummoxed.

"Want some coffee? We can walk down to the study area and grab a cup. I could use a pick-me-up."

As we walked, we talked about history.

"Susan, we can't separate God's timeline from the world's timeline, including our own U.S. history. God created history. It's His story, right? We must not separate the two if we want our kids to see how God still intervenes in everyday events."

"What do you mean?"

"Well, think about it." I poured our coffee, and we added packets of creamer. Preparing the coffee gave me time to shoot an arrow prayer to God, asking for His Words and His help with this conversation.

I continued, "While various civilizations began, thrived, turned from God, and ultimately fell, God was at work. Egypt was experiencing one of the worst famines in its history while Joseph was second in command to Pharoah. The Roman Empire was in control when Jesus grew up, began his ministry, and was crucified. I have to bring up all of history, not bits and pieces of it. And it needs to be taught in chronological order."

"Well, I guess that makes sense. I see your point about two timelines."

"I'm glad you do. And guess what? The same holds true for literature. We can teach any literature, including Shakespeare, from a biblical worldview. In Romeo and Juliet, for instance, we can discuss the importance of relationships and examine what the Bible says about difficult topics such as suicide. And it doesn't end there."

"What do you mean?"

"Okay. Let me give you an assignment, and how about we meet again on Thursday? In the meantime, look up Fibonacci and God's thumbprint. You'll see how intricately woven God is in all subjects."

A couple of days later, Susan and I met again. She had spent some time doing a little research.

"Okay, look. That little assignment was fascinating. I get your point. I just wanted to make sure Linc could think for himself. That he wasn't being told what to think." She smiled. "I see that's what the teachers are trying to achieve—teaching our kids to think critically while emphasizing God in all things."

"We hope that our students here will be influential in our culture—in the arts, business, media, and education, to name a few areas. Why don't you spend some time here and hang out in our classes? Listen to a few lectures. I think it would give you a new perspective!" I hoped she would. Our open-door policy had opened the eyes of several parents.

Susan left that day, and I breathed a sigh of relief. Her son, inquisitive and full of energy, was quite bright—a logical and creative thinker. We needed his Christian influence.

Thank you, God, for being there just when I needed you.

I packed my case and rolled it out the door towards my car, identifying with the Dutch boy who held his finger in the dike to prevent the dam from breaking. Could one tiny school make a difference?

Only with God's help.

CHAPTER 16

Unexpected Battles

"Therefore take up the whole armor of God, that you may be able to with-
stand in the evil day, and having done all, to stand."

–Ephesians 6:13

AS I'VE PREVIOUSLY mentioned, when I was young, I thought of going to the mission field. Back then, I romanticized living in a rural village with friendly parents and a multitude of children and young people. I saw myself as well-received in a relaxed, loving atmosphere while I shared the Gospel.

Clearly, I was naïve.

I hadn't run a ministry until Hill Creek and never thought much about spiritual attacks until then. I had thought the stories about spiritual warfare were conspiracy theories thought up by kookie people. Oh, I knew the Bible talked about them in the book of Ephesians, but that was way back then. It didn't take me long to realize a few things.

While directing Hill Creek, I learned that everyone has an opinion, and if you are the person in charge, dozens perceive that they would do a much better job at running things.

I was often shocked by that realization.

At one conference, while a parent shared her son's high school progress report, we had a mild disagreement.

"Okay, Patty. Jake completed 37.5 hours of grass cutting. I have all the hours documented here." She passed the organized sheet of neatly documented hours across the table, with photos of her son happily riding a lawn mower in one picture and pushing it in another.

I perused the information. "Stacy, thank you for doing such a nice job of documenting hours. We might count this as a quarter credit for physical education if he pushes the mower more than he rides. Is that what you're thinking?"

"Oh, no! He already has all his PE credits! I want to count those hours for science. Biology. He's outdoors in nature, mowing the lawn. The way I see it, you can grant him a quarter credit as a biology credit."

I chuckled, mistakenly thinking she was joking.

"What's wrong?" she asked.

I realized she was serious. I took a breath.

"We can't count these hours for grass cutting as a high school science credit. Hill Creek is required, through Academy Northwest, to follow state requirements. The biology requirements are fairly involved. Let me show you the chapters in the biology textbook." I reached for the textbook from the pile I'd brought to the conference. "I thought I'd shown you this before! If not, I apologize! But it's certainly not too late in the semester to rectify the issue. I'll do everything I can to help you and Jake get on track for his biology credit."

"Well, you did show me that textbook, but I'm not a fan of textbooks! I'm a homeschooler. I like being independent."

Lord, I could use some help. I was getting used to arrow prayers by now.

"How about I show you what a science class would look like for credit?"

Stacy huffed. "I am paying tuition, and I want this credit on Jake's transcript!"

"I wish I could do that for you, but I'm required to follow the graduation guidelines."

Stacy leaped to her feet. "I figured you'd be narrow-minded about this! Here are the hours for his other subjects. Maybe you can count them!" With that, Stacy stomped out of the room and slammed the door.

Until now, I'd thought she and I were on the same page.

After that, to my dismay, she told every parent in the learning center just how narrow-minded I was. She made sure to tell them that they needed to know what their tuition was paying for. It fractured attitudes for a few weeks.

That incident kept me awake at night. I had thought I'd communicated what a biology science credit looked like. Apparently, I had not communicated well enough. Obviously, we had a problem. In the meantime, Stacy decided to homeschool on her own. I was heartsick about that news because I liked her son. Clearly, he was not getting a well-rounded science credit.

This was one of many issues that occurred seemingly out of the blue. It would not be the last.

Not long after the incident over science credit, Amorah and I interviewed prospective teachers. Some we interviewed had taught in a public-school parent partnership homeschool program and were quite popular among parents. I respected them a great deal.

Things went well in the first year or so with our new teachers, but then I noticed a difference in one of the teachers' attitudes at faculty meetings. We couldn't agree on dress code, disciplinary techniques, chapel topics, and history textbooks. Additionally, she wanted the annual school schedule to fit her individual needs. I was surprised that she seemed oblivious that the other teachers had scheduling requests, as well. Amorah and I tried our best to make things work for that teacher and everyone else.

Time rocked on, and the teacher decided not to assist with our extracurricular events, even though she had previously committed. Other teachers followed suit, and soon, the faculty camaraderie plummeted.

I was baffled by the behavior, but I felt we would eventually work things out. Each teacher had signed an agreement saying they would fulfill their duties, including a few extracurricular events. But the atmosphere continued to be unpleasant no matter how hard we tried to make things work.

One day, as I was praying, it came to me that Amorah and I needed help solving this issue. I suggested we add an advisory committee. Amorah, who also had been greatly unsettled by the recent challenges, wholeheartedly agreed. We carefully selected four parents whose children had attended HCC for several years to serve on the committee. Their Christian example and wisdom helped us through that difficult time, and I knew that the issue was resolved due to their wisdom and our collective prayers. It felt good that we could now refer to the "Advisory Committee" when making decisions and solving problems that might arise. Decisions were not just mine and Amorah's, but those of a group of respected Hill Creek parents.

I began to see that we had been in a spiritual battle.

Two gifted teachers left the school. One said she felt she could have run the school better than Amorah or I. Another felt she should have been one of the directors of the school. I agree that both gifted teachers could have done a great job directing HCC, but that wasn't the issue. The issue was submission to the leadership and honoring their agreed-upon contract.

That incident left me wearier than ever. At least I was aware of what we'd experienced—a full-frontal attack on the school. Once I recognized that type of attack, I figured out we needed a prayer team.

But I also realized that I personally needed a strategy for praying.

For one thing, I learned it was imperative that I carve out a specific time to pray. I could only find that time early in the morning, which meant rolling out of bed a few hours before classes started at HCC. It was hard at first, but eventually, I became used to it. I thought of it as having coffee with God.

Learning to fight the spiritual battles took time, but I was beginning to learn. I discovered that my mission field could only be successful if I gave every situation over to God.

Despite what I'd learned, I did not expect the next stage of my journey to be so difficult.

CHAPTER 17

Learning Through Discouragement

"Have I not commanded you? Be strong and of good courage; do not be afraid, nor be dismayed, for the Lord your God is with you wherever you go."

–JOSHUA 1:9

NOT LONG AFTER the previous one, a new kind of attack hit. It was one of personal discouragement, and I believe it was due to weariness. It caught me off guard.

I had been feeling overwhelmed around eleven years into my leadership roles at the school. I struggled to manage parents' needs and the students' issues, minister to the teachers, stay on top of classes I taught, manage the writers' conference, and meet the needs of my own family. I began to think I was not cut out for such a responsible position. Maybe I was not capable or equipped to handle all the problems. After all, I was just a person who loved working with kids. The more I thought about it, the worse things got. Everything was an effort. Even though I loved the school with all my heart, enjoyed working with Amorah, and loved the students, I began to entertain the idea of quitting. Someone has said the battle begins in the mind.

To compound the issues, I had an emergency surgery, and within a couple of months, my father, who had endured quite an extended illness, passed away. As a last resort, he had started kidney dialysis. My husband and I had divided the time taking my father to dialysis three times per week. In the meantime, my mother and our son continued to need extra support.

I went to the doctor who ran tests. She explained that I was suffering from adrenal fatigue, and she suggested I take a break from work.

For the first time, I was not answering emails efficiently, and my response time on answering phone messages lagged. I managed to be ready for my classes but was not handling student problems to my standard. Also, it was the season of the year when we needed to plan for the next school year, and I had reduced energy. I texted Amorah, "I need to talk to you. Can you meet with me tomorrow?"

A few days later, Amorah and I met. "I need to step down as Hill Creek's director. You can take over the learning center. I need some time off."

"What? You can't do that! I can't run the school on my own!"

"Nonsense. You've been teaching students and advising parents for a few years and are smart and organized. Amorah, I've taught you or modeled to you everything I know."

"I can't do it, Patty. I like the way we work together. I can try until you come back. I'll keep it going until you return." We made a deal. Amorah would take over the following fall.

Something felt "off," but I didn't pay attention to the nagging doubt of my decision to leave the school. I felt exhausted and burdened. Maybe God was leading me away. Amorah was young and energetic. Yes, God was probably leading me away.

The school year ended. I'd done my best to set things up for Amorah's success. For one thing, she had a fantastic secretary who was an experienced homeschooler. Also, the remaining English teacher, Lynn, was a seasoned homeschooling parent who had run her own learning center through Academy Northwest.

The following fall, I stayed home while Amorah ran the school. But by January, I realized I'd made a mistake. I was not ready to quit teaching. Now what?

I did the only thing I knew to do. I applied to a couple of places. One was a job at Bellingham Technical College. I knew I was the right person for that job. But I didn't get it. I was surprised, but I decided to apply to Skagit Valley College. That job was a perfect fit, too, or so I thought. The day I went for the interview, I had the flu and should have rescheduled the interview. I didn't get that job, either, even though I'd worked in the same type of job years before. In the meantime, a local public school homeschool program called me every few days asking me to apply. I thought that was strange. I'd never applied to their program.

Eventually, I took the public school homeschool job and met some talented teachers. I threw myself into the job, but my heart was not entirely in it. I was making more money, but that didn't excite me. Money had never been a motivator for me. I told some teachers about Hill Creek, and they applied. I had not taken that job to recruit anyone. But the following year, we were all back at Hill Creek. God had graciously turned my discouragement into something good.

It hit me. I had succumbed to a spiritual attack and, possibly, the oldest one in the book. I had become discouraged. This experience taught me that I should share my discouragement with someone else. But, I believe, due to childhood trauma, sharing deep and personal things has always been extremely difficult for me. In fact, one person had suggested I write a memoir about how HCC began, including the school's history, but I knew I could never be transparent enough to take on that challenge fully.

When I returned to HCC, I agreed to co-direct with Amorah. She was more than capable and competent. I felt co-directing rather than trying to do much of the work myself was the way to go—I knew God had established this new partnership. And it felt good knowing that Amorah could take the school further into the 21st century than I would be able to.

Amorah and I learned through that ordeal that we have an "Enemy," and he never rests.

I learned that our work at HCC was and continues to be a threat to the Enemy, so prayer is key. I also realized that homeschooling works best through partnership with others. Any homeschooling teacher or parent might suffer burnout, and I learned that at the first sign of it, it's a good idea to call on others for support.

I also learned that prayer is not a last resort. It's our first defense. For the Believer, it's our weapon of choice. I've heard it said that the best defense is a good offense. Praying with family, friends, and other like-minded Christians is our most valuable offensive weapon.

Sometimes, we must quit what we're doing; other times, we need to press on. Through prayer, we can differentiate, curtailing our spiritual enemy's attacks.

CHAPTER 18

A Rainbow of Hope

"I dwell in possibility."

–EMILY DICKINSON

I HURRIED INTO the church. My class would begin in a half hour, and I had some setup to do. I put some refreshments in the refrigerator for a scheduled lunch-hour assembly and chapel. The thing I most enjoyed about this church facility was the open kitchen and fellowship hall. Until now, we'd been able to use the kitchen almost anytime we needed it.

At first, I didn't notice the addition of the vast array of rainbow flags displayed around the fellowship hall's great room walls. But shafts of sunlight radiated through sparkling windows, finally capturing my attention. The bright, multi-colored flags in the sun's rays lit up the room. Subconsciously setting aside all thoughts of the upcoming English class I would teach in about twenty minutes, I stood transfixed.

Have you ever experienced a moment so quiet you thought you'd gone deaf? Maybe the whole earth is silenced during those moments. Perhaps only our ears are muffled. Some call it an "Aha!" moment. It dawned on me that the flags weren't celebrating Noah's ark and the covenant of the rainbow—God's promise from Genesis.

The atmosphere at the church had changed a few months before, but I had dismissed the signs. Amorah and I truly appreciated the facility. It was centrally located, and the former pastor, Reverend Blair, had proved gracious and helpful. He encouraged the students, and they respected him. Straightforward, kind, and considerate, he embraced our school. I felt like we belonged.

A few months before, Reverend Blair had walked into my classroom at the end of the day and informed me that he was retiring. He told me there would be no problem with us continuing to rent, but I remember feeling uneasy. Would things stay the same?

A short time later, true to his word, he retired, and the new pastor, Reverend Beck, followed. This new pastor seemed distantly courteous and far more reserved than Reverend Blair.

One day, during a U.S. history lecture, I highlighted a term presented in our textbook—manifest destiny. Manifest destiny was a belief in the 19th-century United States that its settlers were destined to expand across North America. The term, a Christian concept, explains that God ordained the settlement of the West for His glory in order to spread the Gospel of Jesus Christ. I knew the term had been opposed, so we discussed the concept in detail. I made it a point to explain that humanity often carries out God's plan imperfectly, which often causes opposition.

We also looked at some of the documented "miracles" or "divine interventions" that had occurred in the settling of America. We defined "divine intervention" as God intervening in the affairs of mankind and in the destiny of the settlement of the United States. My goal that day was for the students to see the miracles God had performed in the past as the U.S. was settled.

While there are many examples of God's Divine Providence, a

few stand out from the rest. The students particularly enjoyed learning that George Washington remained uninjured on the battlefield on several occasions despite his horse being shot from underneath him, his hat being shot off his head, and his jacket being riddled with holes. They also liked the story of Squanto, who had been taken captive to England, where he subsequently learned English. He managed to voyage back to his native village only to find everyone had died from an epidemic of measles. It so happened that the Pilgrims were nearby and struggling in the New World. Squanto offered to help the Pilgrims by showing them how to plant corn. The fact that he spoke English certainly made communication easier. The students were particularly riveted by the story of seventeen-year-old Sacagawea, married and with an infant son, who assisted Lewis and Clark on their Corp of Discovery journey. Lewis and Clark happened upon a Shoshone band led by none other than Sacagawea's brother, who happened to be the chief. After the emotional meeting, Sacagawea's translations ensured safe passage through the Bitterroot Mountains.

After the lecture, I asked the students to discuss the questions I'd prepared in their designated groups. During the session, I interacted with the various groups. As I approached the classroom's open door, I noticed Reverend Beck standing in the hallway just outside the door, listening to the discussions. I smiled and invited him to come in, but he turned and walked away.

Soon after, I noticed several scheduling conflicts we hadn't previously encountered. Church attendance was small, with few members, and I was surprised when the facility was unavailable for some of the school's special events.

One day, the new pastor informed me that the kitchen had been found in disorder. Parents and teachers regularly ensured that we left things in order, but we had somehow goofed. I apologized to the pastor and promised to rectify the situation. We spent a few hours cleaning the entire kitchen with a few student volunteers, leaving it sparkling. But a few days later, more issues arose. I was dreading inquiring about rental space for the following year.

Forcing myself to the present situation, I considered the rainbow flags. They would distract from today's assembly and the upcoming Awards Night.

Amorah and I discussed the issue and felt we needed to find another venue. But where? In the meantime, I looked for rental space but hit a dead end each time.

One day, I was talking to one of the pastor's wives from my church. She said she thought our church had unoccupied rooms during the week. She suggested that she talk to her husband to see if our school could move there. I was stunned as the thought had not occurred to me.

In a week or so, she got back to me and said she thought it was possible. From there, things were set in motion for the school to move to Emmanuel Baptist Church. Amorah and I were both thrilled. We would have more space and be in a church where our doctrinal beliefs were aligned and where God's covenant with the rainbow would be honored.

CHAPTER 19

The Move to EBC

"To everything there is a season, A time for
every purpose under heaven."

−Ecclesiastes 3:1

I WRESTLED A box of books from my car's trunk. Amorah had pulled up next to me and was doing the same thing. We greeted one another from around the boxes, and headed toward the wide church doors. We paused for a moment. It was a beautiful August day, and the weather was mild. A variety of colorful blooming flowers announced it was still summer, but the changing leaves pointed to fall and the first day of school. I loved that time of year.

I juxtaposed the large church with the one-room schoolhouse and then the smaller church we'd just moved from.

"God has brought us a long way," I practically whispered more to myself than to Amorah.

"Yes, He has!" Amorah was excited to claim her new, more spacious room with plenty of windows and light.

"It's truly amazing that God opened these doors. I wonder what He has planned."

"Well, we won't know until we get started!" Amorah was speeding forward, but I stood another moment, taking in the surroundings. I continued to assess our space once we walked through the open door.

Emmanuel Baptist Church was my home church, so I knew the layout pretty well. The sanctuary was opposite the West Wing, where our classrooms sat empty and waiting. In front of the main West Wing doors was a good-sized foyer. Just beyond that was another set of doors that opened to the vast gymnasium. Three classrooms were to the right of the foyer and down a small flight of stairs. Up the stairs were two other classrooms. The classrooms would certainly meet our needs well. The gym would be used as a study hall and gathering place. We'd section it off—one section for lunch, social time, and study groups, and another for quiet study and tutoring.

Out of the corner of my eye, I noticed a large fire alarm. I wondered if we should practice a fire drill and made a mental note to check with the church administrator.

Just off the gym was the church kitchen. It would be perfect for fundraisers and other school functions. At the opposite end of the church, a hallway lined with pastors' offices opened to a large foyer, with the sanctuary to the right and the church office just off from the foyer. As agreed, we'd have the use of the chapel for special events such as guest speakers, Awards Night, and monthly chapels. Further down the hall, double doors opened to the spacious children's wing of the church. For the time being, that section was off-limits except for our science fair and writers' conference. That was fine with me.

I walked into the classroom designated for my classes and parent conferences and began to set up for the first day. While I was working, I thought about ways we could demonstrate our appreciation to the church. I hoped the students would make a good impression. EBC was a rule-following church, and it was one of my roles to ensure HCC would respectfully follow the rules. After all, that should be easy. Weren't homeschooling students, as a whole, a polite and respectful group?

* * *

The school year started well, and we were sprinting towards a welcome Thanksgiving break. So far, so good at EBC. I was about to wrap up teaching a writing class. I felt good that my quarterly goals for the students were on track. No small miracle. The space at EBC was working well, and the teachers and students clearly appreciated it.

A loud siren blared. I looked at the kids. They looked at me. I mentally scolded myself for not taking the time to discuss a fire drill with the church administrator. Several of the kids jumped up to look out the window. I told them I'd check things out. I rushed out of the room to find other teachers looking similarly confused. No one wanted to give up precious class time to deal with an impromptu fire drill.

"Patty, did you forget to tell us about a fire alarm?" one of the teachers shouted.

I shook my head. "We'd better get the kids outside!"

Just as we herded the last kids outside, the fire department arrived, complete with sirens. The kids talked excitedly. This was real entertainment!

I was called into the gym. *This couldn't be a good thing.*

Firemen, the church administrator, the children's ministry director, and a few pastors were milling around.

"Looks like one of the kids pulled the fire alarm."

One of our kids? Oh, great.

Eventually, all the kids returned to the classrooms. The fire department left, and pastors and others meandered to their offices. The children's ministry director walked up to me smiling.

We walked over to the fire alarm. It would be easy enough to pull the alarm which had been reset.

"Kids will be kids," the children's ministry director said. I felt slightly relieved.

"I suppose," I said. My pride was wounded, and I was disappointed. So much for a good impression. *Would we be invited back next year?*

About that time, the church administrator walked up. "Things are under control," he said. "There could be a small charge for this one since it was unplanned."

"Charge? How much?"

"I'll get back to you on that."

I left the gym to talk to the school secretary. "Would you mind getting the word out that whoever set off the alarm should come to see me in private?"

She said she'd make the announcement right away.

* * *

Thirteen-year-old Cooper and I sat quietly in my room. He'd pulled the alarm. I wasn't the least bit surprised that he'd done it. And I wasn't surprised about why he did it.

Hill Creek, like all schools, attracted all types of learners. In our school, like most, we enrolled extroverts who love being in the front and center of all the activities. We also had a few quiet and contemplative types. There were several kids who were set on achieving scholarships to college, while others planned to work in the family business after a few community college business classes. Some planned to get a job, get married, and start a family right away. One girl in my advanced English class put all her spare time into reading Shakespeare's plays and memorizing lengthy passages. It was a fun pastime for her. Another student had learned from a guest instructor from a local university how to write a good screenplay and create trailers to advertise the screenplay. Some performed in the local community theatre. Cooper was an observer and a thinker whose main focus was technology and how things work. In almost all cases, the students achieved academically.

Coop was an exception. He obediently sat through classes and absorbed the information but rarely completed homework. In fact, my main goal for him at HCC was for him to learn study skills and motivational techniques. His parents expected Coop to mature during the process. Currently, he had decided to read physics books determined to understand the theory of relativity. He often wrote notes on physics topics. During lunch, when I was grading papers or working with a student, I'd have him complete homework that was due. Theory of relativity or not, he did have to meet the requirements of his coursework. I hoped that, eventually, he'd conform. I felt he was bright and could succeed if he would simply complete his assignments.

"So, Patty," Cooper explained, "I noticed the fire alarm when we first moved into EBC. I thought it looked outdated, and that concerned me. I researched fire alarms and deduced that it was no longer operational due to its age. It continued to bother me. I finally decided to pull the alarm to make sure. I figured I'd get an infraction if it went off, but it would disclose a safety issue if it didn't. I was willing to take the risk."

"I see," I said.

He got to the point. "So, what's my penalty?"

"The first thing I want you to do is talk to your dad about it. Better for him to hear it from you than from me. Secondly, I expect you to work before and after school accruing points. Each point equals a dollar. It looks like the fine could be as much as "$75.00. So, 75 points. One hour is one point. Agreed?"

He nodded. Physical work was not a problem for Cooper. It was sitting and doing homework that he was not accustomed to. "Oh, and plan to spend lunch with me doing homework. If your dad agrees, we'll spend an hour after school, as well." He got up to leave.

"And, Cooper, one last thing. If you ever observe again what you deem to be a safety issue, how about running it past me ..."

"Sure thing."

Later, Cooper's dad asked if I would test his son. I told him I thought our annual testing was sufficient, but he wanted Coop's testing individualized.

The results were clear. Cooper was quite bright. We needed to continue to help him achieve.

Eventually, Cooper matured as we hoped he would. But it took time and effort. I couldn't help but wonder, though, how things would have turned out for him in a traditional school setting.

Thanksgiving came and went. The second semester arrived. With the extra space, extracurricular activities, and academic focus, the school year wrapped up on a good note. One school year flowed into the next. The school grew stronger. The community recognized our school. And Cooper, along with his peers, matured.

More Hill Creek teachers joined us. One English teacher, I'll call her Carla White, walked into my classroom one day. Carla was a fantastic English teacher. Committed, talented, and helpful, she was an asset to Amorah, me, and all the students at HCC. And she had never given up on Coop, for which I was grateful.

"I wanted you to read this. It's an essay written by Cooper."

"Thanks. I'll read it right away."

Carla returned to her classroom, and I began to read Cooper's essay. The entire essay was full of insight, but the conclusion touched my heart.

"Like Christian and Hopeful in the Castle of Giant Despair, we can see our own mistakes clearly. Staying on the right path is obviously easier than getting off the path and trying to get back on it. However, we all make mistakes and troubles arise. During those times, it's good to remember to have faith that God will only give us what we can handle and might use troubling times to strengthen our resolve to continue on the right path."

I placed the essay in a folder and smiled. Cooper had indeed heeded his own advice. He had risen above life's challenges with God's help, determined to make a difference by getting on track and staying there.

CHAPTER 20

A Discovery
(The NILD Program)

"Simple can be more complicated than complex. You have to work hard to get your thinking clean to make it simple."

–STEVE JOBS

AS KATIE'S MOTHER left after an hour-long meeting, I wondered if I could find the key to open her daughter's mind to reading, spelling, and writing. We'd never finished what we'd started in sixth-grade language arts class two years ago. The following year, she transferred to a five-day Christian school in our community, but the family preferred homeschooling. Katie was now in ninth grade, and I had agreed to tutor her. Her mother explained that Katie had been in a special program, and it had helped.

Back in sixth grade, this delightful girl had struggled greatly with reading, spelling, and various types of writing, yet she was a good writer and enjoyed writing short stories and children's picture books. Funny and creative, she was a unique learner who had confounded me. Clearly, the traditional approach to learning did not apply to her. I knew there was a way, but I had to find it.

In Katie's sixth-grade writing class, after I'd carefully introduced a concept, she had been unable to answer the basic follow-up questions or begin the assignments without in-depth one-on-one help. Her behavior in class set a good example, and she was popular among her classmates due to her upbeat attitude. She motivated them to work hard. But swaths of concepts missed the target no matter how well she listened and behaved. I realized her ability to take in information was completely different from most other learners.

Writing, for instance, had come to life for her when I introduced a color-coded approach to paragraph writing. She saw the introductory sentence in color. The details were green and blue, while the summary sentence was red. After all, the summary sentence was the end of the paragraph—like a red light. We had made progress in the various types of paragraph writing that year, and we had even delved into basic essay writing.

Katie had been excited about our writers' conference that year. Her adjudicated short story, after much hard work and many edits, had won her a much-coveted place among her peers. It hadn't mattered to her that she didn't win first place. A win was a win, and that confidence builder had encouraged her to write more.

By observation, I knew Katie could be successful. So why hadn't she been able to keep up with regular coursework without an insurmountable amount of effort? By the end of her sixth-grade school year, I felt she'd learned some concepts, but I knew I'd missed the mark with this effervescent twelve-year-old girl. And then she'd gone to another school. I had lost plenty of sleep over that.

Now, I had a second chance. I promised myself I'd get it right this time around no matter what it would take.

* * *

At our first individual session of her 9th grade year, I expected to slog through reading comprehension, vocabulary, and writing responses despite her mother's comments that Katie had improved. Her handwriting had been nearly illegible before, so I knew it was imperative that we work on that, as well.

But to my astonishment, Katie was able to write beautiful cursive handwriting! After a little while, I realized that she could analyze, synthesize, and she could write clear paragraphs. Her reading, I could tell, was near grade level. I was awestruck by Katie's academic metamorphosis after a mere two years.

Someone held the key, and I intended to track down that person.

"Wow, you've improved so much!"

"Yeah. I guess so. But it was awful. At the Christian school, there's a program for students who struggle. I was so scared of my teacher I had to meet with twice a week, but Mom made me stick with it for two school years even though I begged her to let me quit!"

"What kind of program was it?"

"We had to memorize a whole book of random words. A blue book. We worked on 8's on the chalkboard until my brain ached. We did puzzles and some math. With built words with letters. I memorized motifs. My teacher was usually upset when I made mistakes, which I always did. But it helped my handwriting. It helped me learn cursive, too. But I was scared every day I walked into that class."

I pictured Katie walking down a long hallway, her fear rising. Well, the teacher's method had worked. I couldn't argue with that.

"How many were in the class?"

"Just me."

"Oh." *Wow. An individualized program.* "And you can't remember the name of the program?" My heart rate increased due to excitement.

"You'll have to ask Mom more about it, but they called it The

Discovery Program. All I know is it's some type of therapy." She shuttered. Clearly, she did not want to remember the experience.

* * *

Katie and her Mom left our tutoring session that day, and I immediately tracked down the educational institution in Norfolk, Virginia.

"Hello! National Institute for Learning Development. May I help you?"

"Yes, I would like to order your curriculum."

Dead silence. "Excuse me?"

"Curriculum. I'd like to order your curriculum." Another long pause.

"Ma'am, do you have your NILD number available?" The woman on the other end exuded patience and spoke with a polite, Southern accent.

"No, how do I obtain one?"

"Ma'am, you will need to enroll in the Level I training session."

No problem there. "Okay! I'd like to sign up! How many sessions are there?"

"Yes, Ma'am. There are three levels, but before you begin, we must ensure you meet the criteria."

"I have a Master's in education." I felt silly using that as leverage. But I had an innate feeling that it might help me get into a class ASAP.

"Yes, Ma'am. But it's a little more involved. Let me explain... " Good grief. I just wanted to enroll in the class, purchase the curriculum, and move on. I was so busy during that time.

Days later and a couple thousand dollars poorer, I was on an adventure to the first training session. The preliminary six weeks of work would begin online through Regent University. From there, I was required to fly to Boise, Idaho, for the intensive two-week training segment. I was fortunate I didn't have to fly to Virginia, as there was a space open in Idaho.

As I considered my workload, I hoped getting away for a couple of weeks would be the break I needed once the online coursework was completed. I'd taken many educational classes to keep my teaching certificate current. My experience had been that the time spent listening to a boring lecture during the day was worth the quiet time in the evening catching up on paperwork or reading and planning. A little extra sleep couldn't hurt, either.

I had no idea what I was in for.

CHAPTER 21

Boot Camp

"Tell me and I forget, teach me and I may remember,
involve me and I learn."

—Benjamin Franklin

I STAYED AT a Hampton Inn in Nampa, just outside Boise. As I checked in, a woman about my age introduced herself.

"I'm Sandra from Bellingham, Washington. Are you here for the Level I NILD training?"

"I'm Patty. Yes! And I'm glad I have the rest of today to get organized before tomorrow's first class."

"They have a great swimming pool here. Want to get some dinner and get in the pool later?"

"Sure."

After a quick dinner later that day, Sandra and I enjoyed the pool. To my surprise, no one else joined us.

"This will be refreshing after sitting in a class all day," I remarked.

"Doubt you'll have much time for this pool. Maybe an hour next weekend."

"Really?" I doubted what she said.

"I'm a recycle. Trust me, you'll be busy."

"What's a recycle?"

"I didn't make the cut the first time around."

"YOU DIDN'T MAKE THE CUT? Did you lose your money?" I was shocked.

"Well, they gave me a tuition reduction this time."

"A reduction? What happened the first time around?" I knew this woman had taught for years. She didn't seem to lack motivation.

"The coursework is intense, and I had just finished a grueling school year with a few hard things going on in my life. I lacked energy. I probably should have done the training at a different time of year."

I couldn't comprehend that she had taken such measures to get this training and then failed the class!

The following day, we drove our rental cars to the training site. A sign told us which room to enter. On the board, a message said to sit anywhere we'd like. Sandra walked in, and we sat next to each other. We chatted as other teachers and professionals found a seat.

Promptly at 8:00, the instructor, Jim, a stern-looking man in his late fifties, entered. After brief introductions, the class began. One peer was a Ph.D., a few were speech therapists, most had Master's Degrees, and almost all were classroom teachers with various levels of experience.

We each had a thick binder, and Jim began with the first module, explaining the origins of the NILD program.

We took a break about mid-morning, got to know each other better, and enjoyed coffee. Back in the classroom, a note in neat cursive was on the chalkboard. It read, "Sit next to someone you haven't sat next to."

Hmmmm. Okay. But I had gotten to know the teachers around me, and they offered comfort in a new situation. Oh, well. No problem.

Immediately after the break, another instructor, Marcy, pulled a name from a bowl on Jim's desk and said, " Close your binders, please. Sandra, summarize the origins of NILD."

Whoa! I closed my binder, filing through my brain, searching for the information we'd just been given.

Sandra gave a clear and concise summary. I was impressed.

I listened intently for the next two hours as Marcy and Jim presented material using slides, video, and lectures. I took in-depth notes on topics such as "What is educational therapy?" " How is it different from tutoring?" "What is the focus of educational therapy?" "What are your goals as a competent therapist?" "How does educational therapy benefit parents?"

Every topic was intriguing. I drank it in, knowing my name was written on a slip of paper and in a bowl on the instructor's desk. Marcy had pulled out a couple of other names and asked questions. The names were dwindling. It was inevitable that my name would be drawn soon. I felt tense.

After lunch, we walked into the classroom. Sure enough, on the board was another message written in perfect cursive. Sit next to someone you have not sat next to.

There would be no getting comfortable in this class setting.

The afternoon was packed full of information. We discussed students who had struggled in our classrooms and how we had met those students' needs. We read case studies. We, again, differentiated educational therapy from tutoring.

After our afternoon break, a note was written neatly in cursive on the chalkboard. Be prepared to write and present a case study in class tomorrow. Memorize the first ten pages of the Blue Book. Complete the syllabication assignments in your language workbook. Be prepared to defend your answers.

A little after 5:00, Sandra and I walked to our cars. "Clear as to what I meant about not having time to swim?"

"Quite," I quipped.

We rushed through a quick dinner. I entered my hotel room exhausted, but there was no time to lounge around. I needed to get on those assignments if I wanted any sleep.

I turned out my light around 1:00 A.M. How do I remember this? Because it was to be a pattern for the duration of the class. I realized how fortunate I was to be in a time zone just an hour from our Pacific Time. What if I had gone to Virginia? A three-hour time zone difference would be a difficult adjustment with this workload.

The next day, we entered the classroom; a leafy tree was drawn on the chalkboard with its roots exposed. On the roots, written in neat cursive, were the following topics: Visual Processing, Visual Discrimination, Visual Figure-Ground, Auditory Discrimination, and Visual-Motor Integration.

Things were getting exciting! I was going to learn how to get to the root of problems in the classroom, and thanks to Jim and Marcy, I did learn in great detail.

The next class day, we began to learn and master techniques. Promptly at 8:00, Marcy began to explain Rhythmic Writing, a method I didn't yet know would be so helpful for my future students.

I learned that rhythmic writing integrates motor and cognitive functions. It provides for hemispheric collaboration. The results are visual motor integration, better sequencing skills, directionality, better focus, reasonable mental calculation, and better handwriting. It all made perfect sense to me.

Marcy emphasized that left-handed students might require extra practice in this area.

Marcy drew a large 8 on the chalkboard. She instructed us to hold the chalk and chalk holder like a pencil. She began tracing left and right, then reversed the procedure.

"Patty, come to the chalkboard and demonstrate this technique!"

My heart skipped a beat. I am left-handed. *Had she noticed? What a dumb question. Of course, she had.*

I walked to the chalkboard, a little intimidated.

"Follow my instructions and say the directions with a loud, clear voice." She fired the instructions in a staccato voice. "Feet together! Left shoulder down! Elbow down! Hand in the correct position!"

"Left, right, left," I said.

"SHOULDER UP, FEET TOGETHER!

"Right, left, right, left," I continued.

"STOP!"

My head exploded! *Lord, help me!* I hoped He heard my whispered arrow prayer.

"Let's try something different! As you trace the 8, I will give you a math fact. Answer the math fact, and then say your direction immediately. I will also give you a command to reverse your direction."

I took a deep breath. "Left, right, left, right."

"REVERSE!" she commanded. "The product of 11 and 11! REVERSE!"

"121, right, left," I answered, practically breathless.

The instructor drew an 8 on the board and then added one the same size but drawn sideways across the upright 8. This was getting more complicated. I could see the directions were more complex, too. My head was spinning.

Finally, the instructor said, "Nice job. Practice tonight on large Post-it notes that stick to your wall. Until then, work on fluidity. I'll be calling you up again. Now, explain to the class why we use chalk, not dry-erase markers."

I turned, and my anxious-looking peers smiled. "I suppose it's because I felt the directions. There is friction between the chalk and the chalkboard; thus, the connection between motor and cognitive abilities."

"Yes. Now, class, let's move from visual to auditory functions."

I could see why Katie was no friend of educational therapy, but I could already see how each session could benefit a few kids I knew. I'd discovered the key I'd been looking for throughout my entire teaching career.

That night I was on my knees praying I would have the energy to complete the lengthy homework assignments. There would not be much sleep. I was looking forward to the weekend. But the weekend was still a day away.

On Friday afternoon, we were assigned enough work to fill every hour for the following two days. But I was determined to spend an hour in that swimming pool! I called Sandra to see when she wanted to go. We enjoyed that refreshing hour immensely.

The following week, other teachers were called up front and asked to summarize, answer, and defend their answers. They were asked to demonstrate the techniques that we were learning. It seemed every teacher struggled with at least one concept.

On the last day before we were to demonstrate an entire educational therapy session in order to be approved and recommended for the next level, the instructors seemed light-hearted for the first time.

"We've been hard on you. We all have a deficit area or two, and we worked hard to observe you to find your deficit," Marcy said.

"And we put you in uncomfortable situations so that you could understand how a student might feel in the same position," Jim added. "Please don't over-compliment your students for tasks they must master."

"But don't frustrate your students, either," Marcy cautioned.

"Excellent therapists find the right balance between the two," Jim said.

I wondered about Katie's therapist's approach. Katie had become frustrated.

Over the next couple of days, we all performed and observed therapy sessions. Now we'd find out if we'd made the cut or would need to recycle. My anxiety motivated me to forfeit sleep and practice. When I did sleep, I practiced in my dreams.

I held my breath at my exit interview. Jim said, "Patty, we have approved you to move on to Level II. Congratulations!" I was flooded with relief.

Sandra and I walked out to our cars. "Going to take Level II next year?" I asked her.

"Sure," she grinned. "Let me know what dates you're thinking of!"

* * *

"Good morning, National Institute for Learning Development. May I help you?"

"Yes, I would like to order some of your curricula."

"Yes, Ma'am. Do you have your NILD number?"

"Yes, I do," I said.

CHAPTER 22

A Servant's Heart

"But he who is greatest among you shall be your servant."

—Matthew 23:11

"LEFT, RIGHT, LEFT, right..." my NILD student said in a clear, firm voice.

"Shoulder down, feet together, elbow down..." I instructed.

Fourteen-year-old David was on week four of his educational therapy journey, and we were working on one of the several techniques I'd planned for him.

David's mother had called a few weeks before to explore possibilities. She explained that her son had been working with another teacher and had improved, but now he needed more. His teacher had recommended me since we offered educational therapy at Hill Creek. The next evening, David's parents met with me to discuss educational therapy and how it might benefit their son. His parents were quite open about David's academic struggle.

"He's still not over his grandfather's death, and somehow, I think that has affected his academics. Sometimes I don't think I'm over Dad's death, either," Vicki said quietly. We sat in silence for a minute or so. As many of us are, I was also acquainted with grief.

"If he's grieving, he might feel unmotivated. He might be asking himself what's the use of learning," I suggested.

"I think it's a definite possibility," David's dad said. "They were almost inseparable. David's a lot like his granddad."

Vicki and Richard needed direction and support for their son, and I felt educational therapy would be a good start. My plan was that one day, David would take a few classes at HCC.

Thus, David and I were standing in front of a large figure eight, the width of his shoulders and the length of his torso, which I had drawn on the chalkboard earlier. The figure eight motif helps with directionality, focus, processing speed, and a gamut of other benefits. David was tracing the eight with a chalk holder. The friction between his chalk and the chalkboard sent messages to his brain. I was about to learn that it helped with emotions, too.

"Okay. Stop. Now reverse the direction and start over," I said.

"Left, right, left, right . . . I have something to tell you…"

"Let's finish this. Direction."

"lef, righ,"

"Put the T on the end, please". . .

LefT, righT, but I need to tell you something . . . Left, Right. When my grandpa died, I stopped trying. I didn't care anymore."

"David, I'm so sorry! Direction, right!"

"Left. . . he liked to take me fishing. Then he died one night."

"Let's stop there," I said.

David's head dropped a little, but he stood in front of the eight on the chalkboard.

"You want to sit down?"

"No, Patty. Not really." He continued to look at the figure eight.

"It's hard to lose someone you love," I said softly. What a stupid thing to say.

David didn't seem offended. "Yes, it still is. One night, when I was twelve, we got the call that he was sick. I think it was a stroke. They took him to the hospital, and then he had to go to a nursing home. He never got better. And I never got to say goodbye." Tears streamed down David's face.

I'd learned from my own experience that grief attacks when you least expect it.

He was still standing in front of the chalkboard, centered on the 8. I figured, given his age, he'd be embarrassed, but he was lost in thought.

"David, I've lost a few people I love, too. One thing I have learned is to try to remember the really good times and what I learned from that person. It reminds me why I loved that person to begin with. Sooner or later, joy returns. *Please, God, give me the right words.*

"I loved being in the boat with him. He taught me everything about fishing on our trips up to Depression Lake. It wasn't just the fishing, either. We loved being there together. They say the lake is bottomless. Sometimes we'd stand at the shore and just stare at it. He wouldn't say anything. I didn't, either. But we were talking, Patty. Even when we weren't talking. And you know what? We still talk, even though I can't see him."

"What does he tell you?" I asked quietly.

"Well, I don't hear words, I have thoughts, and I know they come from Grandpa. Don't give up. Be patient. Try hard. You know, fishing thoughts."

"Just fishing?"

"What?"

"I was thinking he taught you way more than how to fish, David."

David struggled in a few areas, but maybe because of his struggles, he could sense things others might overlook.

"Educational therapy takes patience, don't you think? It's like fishing. Many times, you have said you're done—not doing it anymore. But then you come back and keep trying. Why?"

"Not sure. Something tells me to keep trying. I want to read better. I want to write a book." He stared at the eight. I looked at him.

"So, you ready to finish up the eights? Get down to business?"

"Left, right, righ, lef, no right. . ."

"Don't forget the T on the end. Think about your direction."

"Okay, Patty."

That was the first of many insights into David's struggles.

The next year, David joined Hill Creek as a full-time student. He went from a lonely and grieving teenager to a connected, engaged, hopeful, and purposeful student.

It wasn't easy. But like a fisherman determined to catch a prize trout, he put his focus, attention, and effort into reaching his goal. He zigged and zagged at times and lost his cool here and there, but he reached his goals because he never gave up.

David left Hill Creek in a better place than when he found it. He volunteered to clean rooms after school and manage the trash. He created a recycling system that worked. I noticed it all, as did others. At times, he could get frustrated, and he struggled to manage his temper, but he eventually learned to maintain control.

I appreciated David's heart. One thing I've learned is that God uses everything, every struggle, every problem. Because of that, David, an extrovert by nature, made friends with many other students. I'm not sure who benefitted the most—David, his friends, or the school. I suspect it was all of that.

At graduation, Hill Creek honors the students, faculty, and especially the graduating seniors. For Amorah and me, those events were bittersweet. We felt thrilled for our students' futures but sad to see them leave.

The year David graduated the chapel was full on Awards Night. We were awarding the Student of the Year, but we'd decided to create an additional award: the Servant's Heart. The Servant's Heart Award would be presented to a student who valued his or her classmates, worked hard to improve the school and student body, and left the school in a better place than he or she found it.

That night, in front of 250 or more students and their families, David was called to the stage to accept the first Servant's Heart Award. For a moment, he hesitated but then walked to the podium to a standing ovation. He seemed bewildered as he accepted the award. Humble people usually are. He had not expected to receive an award other than his hard-earned high school diploma. He was mainly there to cheer on his classmates who would win the awards. I clarified the Servant's Heart criteria and then congratulated David as its first recipient. I mentioned that he would be a tough act to follow.

At the end of the evening, Amorah and I talked with various families. Then we all packed up and cleaned up. It had been another hard but successful school year for so many, and I was blessed to be a part of it all.

Finally, I was able to get to my car. David was waiting.

"Thank you, Patty. I don't know what to say other than thank you."

"You'll be missed, David. I'll imagine you as being on a long, successful fishing trip.

"Yeah, I kind of have the same feeling. But I haven't left just yet."

"You know, David, you only had your grandfather for a few years, but he taught you a lot. From all you've told me about him, I think you've grown into a grandson he'd be proud of."

I hugged him and noticed he had tears in his eyes. But these were not the same tears he had shed in front of the eight's motif. These were tears of joy.

As I drove away, my heart ached. David had graduated and was in the process of launching into his adult life. I knew it would be a journey, as I'd lived it with our son, Justin, and at that time, several others like David and Justin. *Lord, we all put a lot of effort into that young man. I will miss him terribly. How can joy and sadness walk so closely in tandem?*

A thought popped into my head. There will be others. For a fleeting moment, I wondered what retiring would be like. To one day drive away from the school for the last time. I decided to think about that another time.

For now, I wanted to take a few days away from cell phones and email, lesson plans, and conferences. I had a garden to plant, and I wanted to spend some time with my family and dogs. Maybe we'd drive up to the lake. In my spare time, I'd been researching fly fishing. Now, I finally had some time to try it out.

CHAPTER 23

Divine Intervention

"For with God nothing will be impossible."

–LUKE 1: 37

IT ALWAYS TOOK effort, more so than any other job, to steer HCC, even with Amorah and me working long hours together to keep things running smoothly. We had yearly goals for the school and followed the outlined course from September to June each year, but the journey was often riddled with the unexpected. Those unplanned events included, but were not limited to, navigating the economic downturn, organizing and hosting an educational fair for the homeschool community, managing conflict and resolution, and the heartbreak and shock of losing an assistant secretary who died suddenly at age thirty-seven. Unfortunately, the economic impact that stemmed from the housing market crisis a couple of years prior had finally trickled down to affecting our school's enrollment and budget. When we thought we'd escaped the financial crisis, our enrollment plummeted just after new teachers joined us.

The problem? People could homeschool on their own without Hill Creek's support, or they could join the public school homeschool programs at no cost. In times of financial struggle, parents, as we all do, must shave the "extras" from their budgets. Amorah and I knew we needed help. But what could we do?

Amorah and I tossed scenarios around. Would we need to close Hill Creek's doors? That was not an option. Those enrolled were counting on us. But how could we retain our excellent teachers with such a small enrollment?

After much discussion and prayer, Amorah and I decided to host a parent meeting where we would be completely transparent about this new challenge. We planned to disclose our budget so that parents would have a better understanding of our deficit. Parents were sacrificing financially to keep their kids at HCC, and teachers had agreed to take a reduction in pay to retain families. What else could we do?

To be ready for the meeting, Amorah prepared an updated budget while I created an in-depth PowerPoint. We would discuss adding additional fundraisers and a minimal tuition increase. We would also suggest that a couple of parents establish a parent prayer time one or two days a week while the students attended class.

To say that this issue was wearing is an understatement. The school was at year seventeen. Much effort had been invested into growing it, and now we faced an issue entirely out of our control, or so it seemed.

To relieve our anxiety, Amorah and I talked often, sometimes kicking around the same thoughts and ideas. It was always good to work things out together.

While we dreaded presenting the issue of lower enrollment, we tried to stay positive. There could be a few beneficial suggestions or insights at the meeting—something we had not thought of. HCC's homeschooling parents had a tendency to be wise.

In the meantime, through our anxiety, we prayed.

The night of the parent meeting finally arrived. We were one of the largest and most academic extensions of Academy Northwest. Of course, I had informed Academy Northwest of our situation. I found that the other extension centers were low in enrollment and also struggling. Sadly, some had closed. We knew if we could weather this storm, it would encourage ANW, and other centers might also fight to weather the storm.

The meeting opened with prayer. I began the program by explaining the issue. Amorah passed out the budget for the following year, and carefully, line by line, we discussed it, answering questions as they arose. We were not in the red but didn't have much margin. We outlined three possibilities for the school.

We could:

– Add more fundraisers
– Reduce the variety of class offerings
– Discontinue extracurricular events such as the writers' conference and science fair

When we completed our presentation, we asked parents to divide into groups and brainstorm the best approach to keep the school running. We explained that we hoped for new and creative ideas. What happened next impressed me so much I will never forget it. Each group went to prayer instead of immediately brainstorming. And from those prayers came ideas—and an answer.

At the end of the meeting, Amorah and I were amazed when two individuals, one a construction worker and the other a grandmother of an enrolled student, donated checks to the school. We were stunned that they totaled $21,000, which was an amount that would more than keep the school afloat. It had never occurred to us that people might simply donate to the school.

As it turned out, we had one lean year, but by the following year, we had increased enrollment, and the year after, we were back up to speed.

Later, Amorah and I were talking. "We did a good job presenting the facts, " Amorah said.

"Yes, we did. But that's not what saved the school."

"I know," she said softly.

"God intervened. He heard our prayers. He's found a way once again to keep HCC up and running. Amazing to be a part of God's plan in the Skagit Valley, isn't it?"

She nodded. We sat in silence for a moment until I asked, "Why are we so amazed? In the future, let's vow to hold to our faith a little stronger. After all, we'd avoid much anxiety!"

Amorah smiled. "For sure! I guess we'd better get busy. Next year is looming!"

I'm writing this a few years after the crisis, but I still remember the events clearly because I knew then, and so did Amorah, that God saved the school by prompting two generous families to donate the exact amount of money to keep the school doors open. And that was at a time when money was tight for everyone.

I have learned that in every crisis, there is a lesson. From this issue, I was reminded that God knew the solution to our problem well in advance. He had bank accounts full and ready. I also realized that praying expectantly is hard when we are tired and overwhelmed. We try to anticipate how God can answer. If we can't think of a way, we decide our options are scarce. Mainly, though, due to the example set by godly parents, I learned that we don't always need to use our minds to brainstorm. Why? Because the parents' prayers were far more efficient than any brainstorming session ever could have been.

CHAPTER 24

Passing the Baton

"…and let us run with endurance the race that is set before us."

—Hebrews 12:1

TWENTY-FIVE YEARS RIPPLED by like the creek in front of our house. Those years felt more like twenty-five minutes. Was that because building the foundation had been easy? Of course not. I believe the time raced by because Amorah and I were in God's will. We'd been called to the task—me for foundational building and Amorah to continue the race into the future. God had a purpose for HCC in Mount Vernon. We'd been called according to His purpose.

One day, as I was working with an educational therapy student, I received an urgent phone call. My mother was quite ill, and her assistant needed me. Things changed that day. There is a beginning and an end to everything. My time at HCC was drawing to a close, and that was the precise moment when I became aware of it.

Since I'd started the educational therapy program at the school, we'd added two other therapists. The demands of that program had required me to hand over more of my responsibilities to Amorah and others. Still, I was swamped with work, both at school and at home.

Amorah carried a full load, including managing teacher's meetings, teaching, and serving as a liaison between HCC and Academy Northwest, along with a myriad of other responsibilities. Amorah's perseverance, dedication, and devotion to the students were obvious. Most importantly, though, she understood how Hill Creek was different from a typical Christian school, and she understood homeschooling from the ground up. She also had her own three children who would be a part of the school, which assured me that she would continue into Hill Creek's future.

She and I discussed the situation. I would continue working as an educational therapist from my home office for the school. I would also stay on the advisory board that had morphed into a formal Board of Directors for the school. I had promised to help however I could. My "retirement" did not mean I wouldn't be available when needed. But Amorah had a great working relationship with the church administrator, and she had, for the most part, supportive, experienced teachers.

As we made the transition, I knew it would be best for me to be less visible for Amorah to take over completely; otherwise, people would still see me in my same role at the school. I will admit that time was challenging both emotionally and physically to both Amorah and me. I had no idea how difficult it would be to step away from Hill Creek after all the years, and it was not easy for Amorah, either, who was my spiritual daughter. In fact, to my heartache, she felt somewhat abandoned. We had worked together for close to fifteen years.

I knew one thing, though. We could count on God to help us through this new trial. He would take Amorah, the teachers, the church administrator, and the board into the future.

As most had been, my final school year was a relay race. Other therapists had joined the school, and they had a full load of educational therapy students in addition to their regular classes. Enrollment was up. Things were going smoothly. I had written more policies and procedures for the new school board—would the school need or use them? I didn't know, but the foundation was laid. I felt satisfied with that.

At home in the late afternoons, I continued to walk the dike with my dogs. We crossed over the creek by trekking across our neighbor's covered bridge. On those walks, I prayed for the school, Amorah, the teachers, the therapists, the parents and students, and myself for energy and wisdom as my mother's health declined. None of it was easy. But when had anything at HCC been easy?

At last, the end of the school year awards night arrived, as it had every year since 1994. The church sanctuary was filled to overflowing. Amorah, poised and confident, welcomed everyone. I felt hopeful yet sad, juggling an uncomfortable mix of feelings as I spoke to parents and students.

We had carefully planned the program to the most minute detail. The students and teachers had worked hard and deserved to be honored. I was always proud of those events where our faculty, staff, parents, and, most importantly, our students were highlighted.

It was almost the end of the program—just a few more items on the list, and then we could wrap up another school year, my final one at HCC. My soon to be 64 years engulfed me.

Then, a video filled with activities, events, and people from across the years began. WAIT! That wasn't on the agenda, and I struggled to keep my emotions and composure in check. There was applause at the end. Then Amorah beckoned me to join her. I never liked being in the limelight-- everyone knew that; nevertheless, I walked up front. I looked out, and my husband was now sitting in the audience, smiling. I spotted a friend, Lynn, whom I'd taught with for years, who had also joined us with her husband. There were a few former students from the early years! Others had gathered, too. I felt surrounded by love, but my emotions raged. Would I lose composure? I was asked to speak for a minute. I took a deep breath. Then, as Amorah handed me a plaque, I handed her an invisible baton.

* * *

Somehow, Steve beat me home. He knew, having retired from a career in the military, what emotions I was experiencing. He gifted me roses and had prepared an array of hors d'oeuvres. But the best gift that evening was the two of us sitting up late and reminiscing about The Little Red Schoolhouse and all the children who had passed through.

Yes, I had reached the finish line at Hill Creek and had passed the baton to Amorah, who had taken it firmly and was already running the race further into the 21st Century.

CHAPTER 25

And Yet We Are Soldiers

"The smile of God is victory."

–John Greenleaf Whittier

HILL CREEK'S LEAD English teacher called one day.

"Patty, would you be willing to be the keynote for the writers' conference this year?"

"What's the topic?" I asked, hoping it was short stories.

"Memoir."

"Oh. *Why does it have to be memoir?* Well, sure, I can do it. It's in February this year, isn't it?"

"Yes. Does that give you enough time?"

"Of course!"

I got off the phone, and ideas swirled through my head. As previously mentioned, several years earlier, the writers' conference topic had been memoir writing, and the speakers were fantastic. Could I do a good job, too? Maybe I could if I started early. Knowing I'd need help, I called a former student, Renee, who had recently graduated from Hillsdale.

"Want to help me teach memoir at HCC in February? You'll be in town, right?"

"Sure thing! How about we get together and discuss plans!"

So, we'd begun to plan instruction, activities, and break-out groups. It was a good thing we started early. . .

* * *

A month or so later, I lay on the sofa, my leg in a boot, my crutches nearby, the ordeal of doctor's exams and x-rays over. The full impact of the situation seeped into my consciousness a trickle at a time. I'd landed in the hospital due to the break. The torn tendon caused intense pain at times. *What next,* I wondered. But at least I was home and on the mend.

"You're gonna need to cancel the writers' conference." My husband, always the practical one, rarely minced words.

"Um." I couldn't muster anything more.

"What do you mean, 'Um?'"

"I'll think about it, but not now."

"Carla deserves to know right away, don't you think?"

"Can we talk about it later?" I felt more than frustrated. I was caught like a trap in a trap. I couldn't stand breaking my commitment to Carla White, the lead English teacher at HCC.

"Sure. Just thinking ahead."

The next few days presented a legion of people armed with meals, flowers, cards, texts, and phone calls. The camaraderie bolstered me more than I could have imagined. Most of them were former homeschool families.

The pain I managed to ignore during the day stalked each evening as I lay on the battlefield of my sofa. I reached for a weapon, a bottle of acetaminophen, grateful for the defense.

Still, the enemy advanced. I fought back. My will was my shield. Night after night, the battle raged. By day, I was a retired schoolteacher with a fractured leg. By night, I was a combat soldier fighting pain, brandishing my sword hewn from prayer and pills.

It was January, and I was determined to be ready for the writers' conference.

One particularly cold, dark night, my insidious enemy pounced. It raged like a hungry panther intent on devouring. I fought back, prayed, and recited verses. Still, my enemy persisted.

I groped for other weapons of defense and plugged in my ear-buds. I listened to calming nature sounds on my favorite app while someone read a story about Joshua. As the battle raged, my resolve lagged. I considered waving my white flag. Steve could have been right. Maybe I should call Carla. But how could I disappoint her? Three weeks out from the event, I knew she would not find a speaker. She was counting on me.

I envisioned myself limping into the writers' conference on crutches. Most of the kids wouldn't even know me, and that, in itself, felt intimidating. What would they think? I'd look ridiculous!

Maybe Carla could find someone else.

I lay back on the pillow and whispered a prayer into the evening's shadows. As I drifted to sleep, events at Hill Creek from over the years surfaced--events I hadn't thought of in a long time.

* * *

A memory of a cold January day surfaced first. The HCC middle school met in the red schoolhouse on our property then. During a short recess, the kids played outdoors, enjoying the sunshine. A boy picked up a stick and threw it onto our frozen pond. As the stick skimmed to the middle, our delighted Golden Retriever dashed to the end of the pier and jumped, breaking through the ice. She struggled to gain traction to climb out and sank each time. Panicked, I was about to call for adult help when one of the boys dragged the boat from the shore toward the icy pond's edge.

"Don't do that!" My shrill voice startled me.

Jack, a sixth-grade boy, answered curtly. "We have to, Mrs. Huey! We have to save her!"

Two other boys, Luke and Jake, jumped into the boat with Jack, shattering the ice with their oars like Washington crossing the Delaware. They reached the exhausted dog. One grabbed her collar, holding her head above water. The others continued to break a passageway through the ice. The dog survived to the cheering students and assistants on the bank.

That memory faded into another.

Two HCC brothers had just lost their mother to cancer. Before their loss, the brothers' positive attitudes and academic excellence spurred on classmates and teachers. But after the memorial service, the boys returned to school, quiet, distant, subdued. How could anyone comfort them in their grief when reminders of their mom were everywhere, but she was nowhere?

One of the brothers, who served as HCC chaplain then, continued to lead spiritually as he drifted through a fog. He confided that he'd thought of passing on the responsibility to someone else, yet I watched him limp to the end of the school year.

"How did you do it, Thomas?" I asked one winter day a couple of years later over coffee.

"I asked God for help, Patty. And I'd committed, so I had to keep going."

Other memories surfaced.

After a rigorous year of never-ending assignments, science fairs, history days, and writers' conferences, some exhausted students slacked off a few weeks before the last day of school. But nearly every year, when those few students slumped, I noticed a pattern. I'd walk into the study area to see students bolstering each other's resolve. I overheard various conversations with the same message: "Finish strong. There are only three weeks left. You can do it." Almost every time, the exhausted warrior-student crawled to the finish line.

Once, I asked an emotionally and physically exhausted tenth-grade girl who had faced a significant trial that year how she mustered the resolve to finish well. She shrugged. "I decided if everyone else could do it, I could, too. And besides, they were counting on me."

I recalled the struggling students who worked so hard that they earned accolades, including significant college scholarships. One graduating senior caught the attention of the faculty and landed one of the highest awards. As he walked to the podium, I knew that only the two of us and his parents truly understood the extent of his sacrifice and selfless commitment. Later, I asked what spurred him on. He said, "Well, you know it's what we do here at Hill Creek."

More memories wafted in like a pleasant summer breeze. I recalled a ninth grader's triumphant victory over marijuana and the enormous impact that one decision has made on the rest of his life.

I remembered another HCC student, a high school track star, who broke her leg mid-year. She resolved to shake off disappointment by going to the pool daily to practice sprints. She and her teammates won at the state level later in the year. I asked her what had kept her going. She thought a minute and said, "I had to. My team counted on me."

I opened my eyes to a sunrise casting its golden hue. The darkness was gone; I sensed a Presence who brought order out of chaos, calm out of anxiety, and strength out of weakness.

I sat up. It came to me that Hill Creek is no ordinary school. The years there had presented us with friends, laughter, joy, and success. We love celebrating those moments. But hard times are inevitable. During those times, we pulled together like a company of soldiers intent on a joint mission. "Faith to Rise Above Obstacles" is the Hill Creek motto just as surely as "Semper Fidelis" is a Marine's.

As the combat soldiers before me, I would complete my mission. I was a soldier in an elite battle unit following our Commander's lead. I would not contact Mrs. White to cancel my writing conference participation, so I needed to muster up like any good soldier.

To any casual observer, Hill Creek folks might appear as average students, everyday parents, and typical teachers. I swung my legs off the sofa, grabbed my crutches, stood up, and spoke aloud, "And yet we are soldiers."

I prayed for strength and then ordered the pain to surrender. I watched it slink out the door.

Back on the sofa, I picked up my laptop. I'd finish my plans for the conference and be ready. No matter how ridiculous I appeared, I would finish what I'd committed to in typical Hill Creek fashion.

The phone rang. "Hi, Renee! What's up?'

"I know it's early, but would it be okay for me to come over and review our conference plans? I have a few more ideas..."

Renee was an early riser, just like me. This former student, who had also suffered a broken leg once, was a blessing to me!

Sure, come on over. I'll put the coffee on!

A Ministry, At Last

AMORAH AND I were at a local restaurant having breakfast recently.

She informed me that Hill Creek was approved as a full church ministry. "Now I feel the school is more secure, making things feel more permanent."

"Congratulations! What an accomplishment! It has been a long time in coming, Amorah!"

As she talked, all the expectations and requirements for becoming an EBC church ministry came back as if no time had passed. . .

Back then, we presented our PowerPoint to the Elder Board, explaining our program and thanking them for allowing us to rent space from the church. We felt they understood our mission as we had conveyed it. Time passed, and thanks to the church administrator, we were invited to present information about our school to the members of the church one Sunday morning. Both Amorah and I felt it went well. We hoped that, eventually, we could become part of the ministry. It seemed our school aligned with church doctrinal beliefs.

More time passed, and we were invited to an evening Elder Board meeting. I felt anxious. I reminded myself that I needed to trust God to help me through the brief presentation I had been asked to make.

The twelve men were guarded, so I couldn't interpret their expressions. These Christian brothers would decide whether or not we would become a church ministry.

I was organized as I'd spent plenty of time preparing, but I was often lost in thought during meetings. I reminded myself to stay focused because I wanted the Elder Board to see the heart of our school.

As I waited for the meeting, I sensed that the past few years' events had converged in a way I could not have imagined. I realized the Lord had brought HCC to this place of acceptance by the church.

The church administrator told the Board I would explain my motivations for starting Hill Creek, our doctrinal beliefs, and our goals for the school. Everyone looked expectantly at me.

I began, "Actually, Hill Creek began as an experiment. I wondered if motivated, college-bound students and students with special needs could benefit by learning together in the same academic setting given the accommodations needed."

At that point, I gave an overview of some of Hill Creek students' accomplishments. College-bound students had been granted generous merit scholarships to their colleges, while students with significant learning challenges gained confidence and direction for post-high school careers. I also gave an overview of a few mission-minded activities the students had planned.

Before I knew it, the meeting was over. We were informed that the announcement would be on Sunday.

* * *

Amorah and I sat together that Sunday.

"When will they make the announcement?" I whispered.

"I'm not sure," she replied. We sat through the church service. Finally, after the last hymn, we were asked to be seated, and an elder walked up front. He explained to the church that after much prayer and consideration, the Elder Board had voted to include Hill Creek

Christian as a provisional ministry of Emmanuel Baptist Church. During the announcement, I thought that while this was not the exact answer we sought, it was another step in the right direction. Amorah leaned into me. I could tell we were both experiencing a combined elation--the joy of completing one thing and the excitement of something new. The foundation was laid, and Amorah and the teachers would take the school into the future with God's help—a beacon of light in our community.

After church that day, I'd had the afternoon at home. I walked outside to the pond, scooped up trout pellets, then walked to the pier and scanned the landscape. I tossed out the trout food.

A trout hit the food. And then another and another, each creating radiating ripples. I observed the individual pools each trout created and how far each ripple radiated and overlapped one another, creating an even larger ring connecting a circle of ripples that continued throughout the pond. The ripples reminded me of the school and all the radiating ripples of students, events, and activities.

* * *

The waitress walked up and pulled me from my reflections. "More coffee?" she asked. I shook my head.

"So," Amorah continued enthusiastically. "All those years of hard work have paid off! I feel good about where the school is right now. A full ministry of the church! But we can't let our guard down. Patty, please keep praying for us!"

I looked at Amorah from across the breakfast table, her face hopeful and excited for the school's future. Thank you, Lord.

"You can definitely count on that, Amorah." I said.

And I truly meant it.

Author's After Note

"For it is God who works in you both to will
and to do for His good pleasure."

—PHILIPPIANS 2:13

HOMESCHOOLING CHILDREN AND starting a school are equally challenging and rewarding. The days are long, but the years fly by. Many parents say they wish they could do it all over again due to the close family ties cultivated during their homeschooling years.

There is an inexplicable sense of fulfillment when God is involved in our life's work. The feeling of satisfaction that I've seen on parents' faces when their homeschooled children have achieved reflects my own experience. If God calls us to a task, He'll see us through. He'll be in it with us. Sometimes, the more complex a task is to achieve, the more assured we are that God is in the midst of it. At least, that's a lesson I've learned.

The school that began in the Little Red Schoolhouse has moved into the 21st century. Classes are taught from a biblical worldview. This is happening using my personal school experience and a one-room schoolhouse model.

If you are considering homeschooling your children, starting a co-op, or questioning whether or not you want to continue homeschooling, I pray this little book will spur you on.

For more information or assistance, visit **hillcreekchristian.org.**

Questions For Discussion

Finally, brethren, whatever things are true, whatever things are noble, whatever things are just, whatever things are pure, whatever things are lovely, whatever things are of good report, if there is any virtue and if there is anything praiseworthy—meditate on these things.

–Philippians 4:8

1. After reading Chapter 1, *Pure Gold*, can you think of one person who motivated you to do your best? How did that person inspire you? Discuss this around the dinner table this evening.

2. Knowing that there are homeschool programs explicitly designed to help you set up and teach your children, will you consider getting started? What steps will you take to accomplish your goal?

3. In your life experiences, what is one path you never thought you'd take but did? How did it change you? Take a look at Romans 5:1-5. Does that passage encourage you? Why?

4. After reading chapter 8, *The Heart of the Matter*, do you think homeschooling or private Christian school is a possibility for you and your family? Why or why not?

5. In chapters 14 and 15, you read that I became discouraged and ultimately stepped down from running the school briefly. Have you ever been so discouraged that you wanted to quit doing something you loved and felt called to? Something worth the effort but caused you difficulties to the point of feeling exhausted and overwhelmed. Do you believe that God can help you reach your goals? Take a look at Matthew 11:28-30. What did you learn?

6. After reading chapters 20 and 21 about Patty achieving an educational therapy certificate, can you think of a time when you signed up for something that required more effort than you intended? What helped you stick to your commitment and achieve your goal?

7. In chapter 22, *A Servant's Heart,* you read about a young man who turned his grief into something good. How can you turn your complex issues into joy?

8. After reading chapter 23, *Divine Intervention,* can you think of a time when God intervened to fix a problem that seemed beyond repair?

9. In chapter 24, *Passing the Baton,* Amorah accepted the baton. When have you received a baton and moved forward with it?

10. In chapter 25, *And Yet We Are Soldiers,* you read about Patty's will to follow a tradition. What traditions do you carry on in your family and life?

How Can I Truly Know God?

Dear Reader,

Maybe you believe in God but want to know Him. Is it possible to have a true, honest, and meaningful relationship with Him?

There are verses in the Bible that are key to knowing God:

God loves all of us

For God so loved the world, that he gave his only son, that whoever believes in him should not perish but have eternal life.

—JOHN 3:16

We are all sinners

For all have sinned and fall short of the glory of God.

—ROMANS 3:23

As it is written: "None is righteous, no, not one"

—ROMANS 3:10

God offers a solution for our sin

For the wages of sin is death; but the free gift of God is eternal life in Christ Jesus our Lord.

—ROMANS 6:23

But to all who did receive him, who believed in his name, he gave the right to become children of God.

—JOHN 1:12

You can be saved!

Behold, I stand at the door and knock. If anyone hears my voice and opens the door, I come in to him and eat with him, and he with me.

—REVELATION 3:20

For "everyone who calls on the name of the Lord will be saved."

*–*ROMANS 10:13

But these are written so that you may believe that Jesus is the Christ, the Son of God, and that by believing you may have life in his name.

*–*JOHN 20:31

Talk to God

Anyone can talk to God as He is a real person. You might say something like the following:

God, I know I am a sinner and I confess my sin to you. I need the salvation you offer. I believe with all my heart that Jesus died on the cross to take away my sins. He rose again to bring me new life. I ask you to forgive me. I want to follow You as my Lord and Savior. Amen.

Once you have prayed the prayer, you are saved. The next step is to prayerfully find a church. The church is the Body of Christ. It is good to gather for worship with like-minded people.

Assurance of Salvation

The Bible assures us of our salvation.

Because, if you confess with your mouth that Jesus is Lord and believe in your heart that God raised him from the dead, you will be saved.

*–*ROMANS 10:9

Truly, truly, I say to you, whoever hears my word and believes him who sent me has eternal life. He does not come into judgment but has passed from death to life.

*–*JOHN 5:24

Commit

Commit to reading the Bible, God's Word, daily to grow in your Christian walk. You can find Bible reading plans on the internet.

God bless you!

About the Author

PATRICIA (PATTY) HUEY was born in the Pacific Northwest but was raised in the South. She began her forty-year teaching career after obtaining a BS in Education from the University of Alabama in Birmingham. Later, she received a Master's in Curriculum and Instruction from Lesley University in Cambridge, MA. In 1994, she founded  Hill Creek Christian in Mount Vernon, Washington, nestled in the Skagit Valley.

As a freelance writer, Patty regularly contributes to the Grace Publishing *Short and Sweet* series and is currently writing nature-based devotions. She is also writing a book titled *Tripp's Time Travels*.

She enjoys meeting with her Christian writers' group, Pond and Parchment Guild, observing wildlife, and spending time with her family and two dogs.

For writing updates, questions, or to leave comments, contact her at mountainpoet@protonmail.com.